How to Worship
Jesus Christ

How to Worship
Jesus Christ

Experiencing His Manifest Presence Daily

Joseph S. Carroll

MOODY PUBLISHERS

CHICAGO

All Scripture quotations, unless otherwise indicated, are taken from the *New King James Version.* Copyright © 1982 by Thomas Nelson, Inc. Used by permission. All rights reserved.

Scripture quotations marked KJV are taken from the King James Version.

Scripture quotations marked NASB are taken from the *New American Standard Bible®*, Copyright © 1960, 1962, 1963, 1968, 1971, 1972, 1973, 1975, 1977, 1995 by The Lockman Foundation. Used by permission. (www.Lockman.org)

Edited by Jim Vincent
Interior design: Ragont Design
Cover design: Smartt Guys design
Cover photo: Con Tanasiuk / Thinkstock

Library of Congress Cataloging-in-Publication Data

Carroll, Joseph S.
 How to Worship Jesus Christ : Experiencing His Manifest Presence Daily / Joseph S. Carroll.
    pages cm
ISBN 978-0-8024-0990-4
1. Prayer--Christianity. 2. Worship. 3. Jesus Christ. I. Title.
BV210.3.C37 2013
248.3--dc23
                    2013014297

We hope you enjoy this book from Moody Publishers. Our goal is to provide high-quality, thought-provoking books and products that connect truth to your real needs and challenges. For more information on other books and products written and produced from a biblical perspective, go to www.moodypub1ishers.com or write to:

Moody Publishers
820 N. LaSalle Boulevard
Chicago, IL 60610

1 3 5 7 9 10 8 6 4 2

Printed in the United States of America

*This book is for
"The Team":*

*Mabel, Elizabeth,
Anna, and Paul*

Contents

Foreword

To Martha, worried and fussing with many pressing chores, our Lord said, "Only one thing is necessary" (LUKE 10:42 NASB).

Worship is that one essential activity that must take precedence over every other duty of life.

Most people, unfortunately, are exactly like Martha —preoccupied, distracted, too busy serving to sit at the Savior's feet. Living in a high-tech age, we tend to be driven by time clocks, deadlines, schedules, appointments, obligations, assignments, and urgent things beyond our control. Few people feel they can afford to put worship at the top of their "To Do" list.

The truth is, we can't afford not to. Worship is ultimately our first priority. Nothing on anyone's agenda is more important. In fact, the hectic pace of modern life only elevates the importance of active, deliberate, purposeful, daily worship of the Lord Jesus Christ.

Joseph S. Carroll understands that priority and has given the church a valuable and practical handbook. In *How to Worship Jesus Christ* he carefully and clearly sets forth the principles of worship—what it is, why it is so critical, and most significant, how to worship.

Joseph Carroll is obsessed with worship and with the glory of our Lord. That comes through clearly in his writing. Worship is his consuming passion, and he wants to set his readers' hearts aflame with the same yearning to know and adore the Lord Jesus. Be prepared to catch his zeal.

Nothing is more sorely needed in the church today than a renewed emphasis on worship. Sadly, the prevailing winds seem to be blowing exactly the opposite direction. The popular themes in Christian publishing appear to be self-help, self-esteem, self-love, self-fulfillment, self-development, and other self-oriented fashions. Even the "deeper life" literature is tainted with an intense self-focus, promising victory, fulfillment, contentment, and other human-centered goals. Those things are fine, even desirable, but they're the by-product of a life lived for God's glory.

Joseph Carroll knows that and rightly fixes his focus heavenward. His concern is not temporal, earthly, or emotional blessings. He is absorbed with the privilege and duty of authentic worship. He understands that the blessings flow from that, for it is only in worshiping Jesus Christ that the believer can both plumb the depths and explore the heights of the abundant life our Lord makes possible.

"But an hour is coming, and now is, when the true worshipers will worship the Father in spirit and truth; for such people the Father seeks to be His worshipers. God is spirit, and those who worship Him must worship in spirit and truth" (John 4:23–24 NASB).

JOHN MACARTHUR
Author of *The MacArthur New Testament Bible Commentary*
Speaker on *Grace to You* radio program

Introduction

This is not a comprehensive treatise on prayer. It deals with one aspect of it. The masters who have given themselves to prayer agree, without discord, that the most important element of all is the essential of worship.

Young people today are not willing to settle for creeds. They want to know the Christ of the creed. Worship is the key to their quest. C. S. Lewis confirmed this conviction when he said, "It is in the process of being worshipped that God communicates His presence to men."[1] And yet, this vital truth has been neglected.

The beloved author and pastor A. W. Tozer in his unique way tells us that

> man was made to worship God. God gave to man a harp and said, "Here above all the creatures that I have made and created I have given you the largest harp. I put more strings on your instrument and I have given you a wider range than I have given to any other creature. You can worship Me in a manner that no other creature can."
>
> And when he sinned, man took that instrument and threw it down in the mud and there it has lain for centuries, rusted, broken, unstrung; and man, instead of playing a harp like the angels and seeking to worship God in all of his activities, is ego-centered and turns in on himself and sulks and swears and laughs and sings, but it's all without joy and without worship. . . .

Worship is the missing jewel in modern evangelical-
ism. We're organized; we work; we have our agendas.
We have almost everything, but there's one thing that
the churches, even the gospel churches, do not have:
that is the ability to worship. We are not cultivating
the art of worship. It's the one shining gem that is lost
to the modern church, and I believe that we ought to
search for this until we find it.[2]

This volume is sent forth with the prayer that it will
be used to end the search for the "how" of worship for
many.

Two worshipers of Jesus Christ, Barbara Haley and
Dorothy King, exercised a faithful labor of love to make
this volume a reality. Indeed, it would not have been published but for their commitment.

Notes

1. C. S. Lewis, *Reflections on the Psalms* (New York: Harcourt,
   Brace, Jovanovich, 1958), 93.
2. A. W. Tozer, *Worship* (Harrisburg, PA: Christian Publications,
   1961), 12, 23–24.

Jesus, I am resting, resting
In the joy of what Thou art;
I am finding out the greatness
Of Thy loving heart.
Thou hast bid me gaze upon Thee,
And Thy beauty fills my soul,
For by Thy transforming power,
Thou hast made me whole.

～

JEAN S. PIGOTT

One Thing Needful

Worshipping God is the great essential of fitness. If you have not been worshipping . . . , when you get into work you will not only be useless yourself, but a tremendous hindrance to those who are associated with you. —OSWALD CHAMBERS

In the evangelical missionary world, there is no name more revered than that of Hudson Taylor. Hudson Taylor, a remarkable man, was the father of modern faith missions. The two volumes of his life by his daughter-in-law are possibly the two greatest works on missionary activity ever written: *The Growth of a Soul* and *The Growth of a Work of God*. What was it that made Hudson Taylor the man he became and was, right to the end?

His son and daughter-in-law, who traveled constantly with him in his later years, testify that often they would be traveling over a hard cobblestone road for many hours in a springless cart. Arriving at a Chinese inn late at night, they would endeavor to obtain a little corner in a room for their father, Hudson Taylor; for usually in those inns there was just one large room where everybody slept. He was now an aged man; but, without fail, every morning just before dawn there would be the scratching of a match and the lighting of a candle, and Hudson Taylor would worship God. This was the key to his life. It was said that even before the sun rose on China, Hudson Taylor was worshiping God.

Lessons from Taylor and Tozer

What did this great man write concerning missions? Did this master missionary, who understood indigenous principles, give us a great volume on the "how" of missions or on the "how" of planting churches? No, he did not. He gave us a very small book, a commentary on the Song of Solomon!

What was the key to Hudson Taylor's life? He loved his Lord, and he cultivated that love. After all, it is the first commandment. Love can only be cultivated adequately in aloneness with the one you love, and this Hudson Taylor guarded.

I have had the privilege of listening to most of the men who would be considered the great preachers in the world today. One, who is now with the Lord, was A. W. Tozer. Dr. Tozer, who labored in Chicago for many years, was different, for he spoke with a freshness and with a penetration that was most rare.

When an acquaintance of mine, who was called to minister in Chicago, arrived in that city, A. W. Tozer called him and said, "This city is a devil's den. It is a very difficult place to minister the Word of God, and you will come up against much opposition from the enemy. If you ever want to pray with me, I'm at the lakeside every morning at five-thirty. Just make your way down and we can pray together."

Not wanting to bother the great man as he was seeking the Lord, my acquaintance did not immediately accept his offer. But one day he was so troubled that he made his way very early to the lakeside, about six o'clock, only to find God's servant prostrate upon the sand, worshiping God. Needless to say he did not disturb him.

A. W. Tozer worshiped God and was one of the few men who preached consistently on the need to be a worshiper of God, telling the church in no uncertain manner that worship was the missing jewel in her crown.

Other Lessons in Worship

I came across the necessity to worship, as the man in the world would say, "by accident"; but it was by God's appointment. In the early days of my ministry in Australia it was my habit when in the city of Sydney to meet with a number of brothers in Christ for a day of prayer. We would begin about eight o'clock in the morning; and because the afternoon was usually a time of tiredness, we would pray around in our circle. When it came my turn one afternoon, I was very tired and began to quote Psalm 19:1–3:

> The heavens declare the glory of God; and the firmament shows his handiwork. Day unto day utters speech, and night unto night reveals knowledge. There is no speech nor language where their voice is not heard.

Suddenly I was quickened by the Spirit of God and began to pour out my heart in prayer. I had not prayed like that all day. I had offered many prayers, but this was different. When I finished and the others were praying, I did a lot of thinking and waiting upon the Lord. What had I done? I had begun with these verses worshiping God from the Psalms; so the next time around I did the same thing, and the same thing happened. I was quickened by the Spirit of God, and there was that outpouring in intercession. I was borne along by the Spirit of God. I knew then that I had been introduced to a priceless key, one that would introduce me to hitherto undreamed-of heights of fellowship with my Lord.

The best time to worship is, of course, in the morning, in that time that we call a quiet time. But what is a quiet time to you? To me as a young Christian, in the early years, it was anything but a relaxed, meditative time. In fact, it was a time when I had to get through a certain study of the Word of God and certain prayers that I had to pray from my prayer list. Thus, my quiet time was not really a quiet time. It was a study time, a time for intercession, a time for petition.

Then I was introduced to a small volume on prayer by A. T. Pierson that led to an intensive study of the teaching of our Lord on prayer. If you collate all our Lord's words on prayer you will find that He taught ten lessons. At the Evangelical Institute where I teach our course on prayer, these ten lessons are the foundation of all else.

You will also discover that you cannot advance from one lesson to another until you master the preceding one. In other words, you cannot go to lesson two until you have mastered lesson one. You cannot go to lesson three until you have mastered lesson two.

Our Lord's first lesson on prayer is found in Matthew 6:6: "When you pray, go into your room ["closet" KJV], and when you have shut your door, pray to your Father who is in the secret place; and your Father who sees in secret will reward you openly."

He is saying, "The first thing you must do is get somewhere alone with Me," for a closet is a closed place. A room can become a closet. It means aloneness. A forest can become a closet. The important thing is aloneness, in secrecy, being alone with your Father.

"And when you have shut your door, pray to your Father who is in the secret place; and your Father who sees in secret will reward you openly." Now, what would this mean to those to whom the Lord uttered these words? To the Jew, the place that was more enclosed than any other and that would immediately come to his mind was the "Holiest of All," that innermost court of the tabernacle and the temple where the high priest met alone with God once every year. It had no door, no skylight, no window. It was completely enclosed.

The high priest went into the closet and stood before God, and it is neither intimated nor suggested that he ever spoke a word. Prayer is a thing of the heart, expressed before uttered, for God looks on the heart.

The high priest stood in the presence of God and communed with Him on the basis of a blood-sprinkled mercy seat, bringing back from that communion a message for the people. What is the first lesson to learn? It is aloneness, secrecy, communing with God on the basis of a blood-sprinkled mercy seat.

How do we commune with God? The writer to the Hebrews tells us that we commune with Him on the basis of a mercy seat, even Jesus Christ who is our Mercy Seat. He is the Lamb of God, our new and freshly slaughtered Way.

Martin Luther said, "It seems but yesterday that Jesus died." What made this great, fearless servant of God so dynamic, so effective? He was conscious that he walked and lived in the presence of the Lamb of God who had been slain for him, for he knew what it was to come by the blood of Jesus and to meditate upon the slain Lamb of God.

We enter into the holiest, into the very presence of God, by the blood of Jesus to commune with Him on the basis of a blood-sprinkled Mercy Seat. That Mercy Seat is Christ Himself, whose blood gives us access.

What did this do for my quiet time? It absolutely revolutionized it. Instead of looking at my watch and saying, "I have ten minutes to get through my prayer list," I simply knelt down and quietly meditated upon the fact that I was in the presence of the Lamb of God and worshiped Him. My quiet time then became something for Him, not something for me; and with the worship of my heart—the pouring out of my heart to Him in worship— came the overpowering awareness of His presence.

During our years in Japan I had a friend with whom I often labored. He had a Renault, a small car manufactured in France, in which he made his way around Tokyo. In those earlier days, the Japanese were most anxious to get you to buy their gasoline. When you pulled into any station, a whole army of attendants would descend on you. One would wipe your windshield, another would check your engine and water, yet another would check your tires, while the final attendant was busy with a little broom sweeping out your car. You just had to get out of their way.

As my friend Julius was driving along in Tokyo, he saw a little light blinking on his dashboard and knew he was short of oil. When he pulled into a gas station and got out of his car, this great army descended, washing, wiping, cleaning, everything. Then he drove out of the gas station and "blink, blink, blink." The team had checked the water in his radiator and the air in his tires, filled his tank with gas, swept out the car, washed the windshield, *everything but that which he wanted.* Is that your experience with the Lord? Do you do everything but that which He wants you to do?

He is seeking us for what? He is seeking us that we might worship Him. That is what the Word of God says. He wants us to study, to pray for others, to give to missions, to go where He directs. But what must precede this? Let us observe Oswald Chambers's significant word:

> Worshipping God is the great essential of fitness. If you have not been worshipping . . . , when you get into work you will not only be useless yourself, but a tremendous hindrance to those who are associated with you.[1]

What would you say if you were asked, "What is the one thing needful, the one thing to really concentrate on in your Christian experience above all else?"

If you are a Baptist you might say, "Soul winning"; and that is admirable. "Soul winning, witnessing, getting others into the church is the primary thing, the one thing needful. If I maintain my passion for souls in my witnessing, all else will be well."

If you are a part of a Pentecostal group you might say, "The fullness of the Spirit, the baptism of the Spirit, is the one thing needful."

If you are Episcopalian you might say, "The one thing needful is reverence for God." Instead of considering the difference in emphasis in denominations, let us consider the Word of God. I believe we can prove from God's Word that which is the most needful in the experience of every disciple of Jesus Christ.

David's Passion

In Psalm 27 we read about David's experience. David was a truly remarkable man, an amazing servant of God. If you are fascinated by preaching, here was a great preacher. If you are inspired by a great leader, here was the great leader of the nation of Israel. If you are interested in soldiering, here was the great soldier, the unconquerable leader of Israel in battle. If you are interested in kingly qualities, he was a great king, the greatest king ever to sit on the throne of Israel. He was an amazing man, "a man," we are told, "after [God's] own heart" (1 Samuel 13:14), a wonderful man of many gifts who commanded the affection of a whole nation and led them to victory again and again. But, of course, we think of him primarily as the incomparable psalmist.

You might have asked David, "What is your ruling passion? What is that for which you live? What is it that dominates you, David? What is the mainspring of your life, the great objective of your life? Is it to be a great preacher, to convert sinners?"

He would have said, "No, not at all."

"Well, David, your passion must be to remain undefeated on the field of battle, to lead your men again and again to victory."

"Not really."

"Is it to rule as a great king, to sit on the throne?"

"Oh no, not at all."

"It's not your ruling passion to be a great king?"

"No."

I think he might have said, "It is rather incidental!"

"Incidental that you are a king?"

"Yes, comparatively."

"Well, David, what is your ruling passion?"

We have his answer in Psalm 27:4: "One thing have I desired of the Lord." David desired only one thing, that was all; but if he had this, all else would follow.

"One thing have I desired of the Lord, that will I seek: that I may dwell in the house of the Lord all the days of my life, to behold the beauty of the Lord, and to inquire [or to meditate] in His temple."

There you have it in one verse of Scripture. There is only one thing he desired; but because he desired this one thing, all things became possible. This is the mainspring. This is what sets everything else in motion and enables all else to function as it was intended and to fulfill its appropriate role. If the one thing that is needful is desired and sought, everything else will fall into its proper place and will perform its proper function.

In a certain city in the southern United States, I recall on one occasion looking at my watch and thinking, "It's rather early." About ten minutes later I looked at my watch again. It was the same time. My watch looked the same—same hands, same case—but it was useless, for it had ceased to function as the maker intended. The mainspring had snapped. The one thing needful had ceased to function.

Keil and Delitzsch in their great commentary have this to say about David's desire:

> There is only one thing that he desires, . . . an ardent longing which extends out of the past into the future, and therefore runs through his whole life. The one thing sought is unfolded . . . a lifelong dwelling in the house of Jahve, that is to say intimate spiritual intercourse . . . is the one desire of David's heart, in order that he might behold and feast upon (of a clinging, lingering, chained gaze) the pleasantness (or gracefulness) of the Lord.[2]

I am quoting from a commentary that is regarded by most conservative scholars as one of the finest on the Old Testament. What is being said? David's desire is an ardent longing that runs out of the past into the future. It is not a momentary thing. Intimate, spiritual intercourse is the one consuming desire of his heart, and it was this that dominated David all his days.

Is that not surprising? David is a man's man, a great soldier, a king of kings, and what does he want to do? The one thing he wants is to behold the beauty and the pleasantness of the Lord. Everything else is relatively incidental: being a great leader, being a great king, being a great preacher, being a great psalmist. Only one thing really matters—intimate fellowship with his God. To be a true worshiper of God is his passion.

But then he says, "That will I seek after." Because this was the primary thing, he knew very well he would never be able to achieve his objective unless he really sought for it; nor will you, my friend; nor will I. At the end of the day ask yourself what you have done with your time. How much time did you set aside to worship Jesus Christ? You might be surprised.

Of course, to worship Him in your quiet time is not the end. It is only the beginning. You are merely tuning your instrument to face the day. We seem to have the strange idea that if only we can have a quiet time, everything is going to be fine for the rest of the day; and if we do not have a quiet time, everything is going to turn out miserably. This is not so. The quiet time should be set aside early in the morning, but it is only the tuning of the instrument. You cannot say, "I have had my quiet time. Now I'm fine." This is just the beginning, getting in first gear, so to speak.

We must walk in fellowship with the Lord throughout the day. C. H. Spurgeon said he was never out of
vital contact with God for more than ten minutes! Little
wonder that God used this great lover of Jesus Christ so
mightily. Like King David before him, C. H. Spurgeon
purposed in his heart to seek to be a true worshiper of his
Lord, for no man will ever experience true worship in a
consistent manner unless he sets his will to do so.

Paul's Passion

What was the passion of the apostle Paul? His ruling
passion is plainly revealed in Philippians 3:10: "That I
may know Him, and the power of His resurrection, and
the fellowship of His sufferings [intimate fellowship],
being conformed to His death."

Now what does "that I may know him" mean? Did
Paul not know Him as Lord and Savior? Yes, but his
ruling passion was to know Him ever more intimately. To
know Him was the primary thing in the life of the apostle. Is "that I may know him" primary in your life?

The apostle could say in Philippians 3:8, "For [Christ]
I have suffered the loss of all things . . . that I may gain
Christ."

Christ was his goal. To win Christ, to know Christ, to
love Christ, to have intimate fellowship with Christ, this
was his ruling passion. If that is not central, then duty becomes a drudge, a chore; but when Jesus Christ is central
in the life, duty is a delight.

This is a day when we have become very clever at de-
veloping techniques, a day when we are apt to be urging

people to witness; and what usually happens? They witness for a while, and then they stop. Then they are exhorted to witness again, so they go a little further, then stop again. But why do they stop? Have you ever noticed in the Pauline epistles that Paul never urges Christians to witness, nor has he anything to say about foreign missions? Nothing! How interesting! If you have to constantly be telling people to witness, something is wrong with them. If you always have to be pumping up people to get them interested in foreign missions, something is wrong with the people. What is Paul always doing? He is consistently bringing you to Christ and leaving you with Christ.

When Christ is central in the heart of the man, what does the man want to do? He wants to tell others about Jesus, and he will do so effectively. Let Jesus Christ be central in the heart of a man, and he is going to be burdened and troubled because millions have never heard of Christ. It is going to disturb him and bring him into action. What he needs is not more exhortation; he needs Christ. And the Christ within him who died for the world will speak through him to that lost world. Without true passion for Christ, nothing works consistently. It loses its power.

Jesus Christ was central in the life of the great apostle.

Mary's Choice

Now it happened as they went that He entered a certain village; and a certain woman named Martha welcomed Him into her house. And she had a sister called Mary, who also sat at Jesus' feet, and heard His word. But [and it is a big "but"] Martha was distracted with much serving, and she approached Him and said, "Lord, do You not care that my sister has left me to serve alone? Therefore tell her to help me." (Luke 10:38–40)

Here is Jesus' answer: "Martha, Martha, thou art careful and troubled about many things: But one thing is needful: [Now underline that. These are the words of our Lord: "one thing is needful."] and Mary hath chosen that good part, which shall not be taken away from her" (10:41–42 KJV).

Here we are introduced to two sisters who were both very busy. You must not think that Martha alone is busy. Mary also is busy, but concentrating on a different form of service.

When the Lord comes to the house, note carefully Martha's attitude toward Him. It is revealing. "Lord, don't You care that my sister has left me to serve alone? Don't You care? You come into the house, You see what is happening, You see I'm doing all the work, and You don't care. Mary isn't doing anything!"

So the first thing we notice about Martha is that she has a complaining spirit. In other words, she is prey to self-pity. If she complained to the Lord and rebuked Him, I wonder what she would do to others in the house?

Then she gives Him a command. Quite a girl, Martha. "Tell her to help me. Don't You care?"

What does the Lord do? He completely ignores what

she has said. He does not say to her, "Now, Martha, I know that you are very busy, and it's just too bad that Mary isn't helping you." Oh, no, He is not going to feed that monster Self in Martha, and He will not feed that monster Self in us either. But if we do not keep close to the Lord, we will fall into self-pity and a complaining spirit.

But what does He say? "Martha, Martha, you are worried and troubled about many things." Underline "things," for "many things" can infiltrate into a dear woman's life and trouble her! We must take what the Lord gives us and be content. *Things* can smother you. They are smothering Martha. Be content with Him, not with things; for did not the apostle Paul say, "I have learned in whatever state I am, to be content" (Philippians 4:11)?

Live for the Lord, not for things.

Our Lord refers to Mary in verse 42 (kjv): "But one thing is needful: and Mary hath chosen that good part, which shall not be taken away from her."

What is the difference between Martha and Mary? You hear some people say, "Well, Martha is a choleric, the activist. She is the person who works with her hands. Mary is different. She is the melancholic: the quiet, introspective, meditative type. They are two different types. So, Martha is obviously going to be an activist, and Mary is going to be given to meditation."

Scripture does not say this. What does the Scripture say? There was a time in Mary's life when she had made a choice, and Martha had not. That is the difference. Mary had chosen, and that is always the difference between the person who is satisfied with Christ and the person who is dissatisfied with life. One had made a choice; the other had not.

How often women come to me and say, "Mr. Carroll, you know I'm a Martha. The kitchen is my place. The home is my place, looking after my family. I'm a Martha."

I reply, "No you are not, my friend. You have chosen to be a Martha. God wants you to be a Mary."

You never drift into being a Mary. You can always drift into being a Martha. All you have to do is just let yourself go. No woman ever drifted into being a Mary.

"Oh, but you don't understand, Mr. Carroll. You don't understand my responsibilities."

I understand them very well. I have lived in literally scores of homes in the forty years of my ministry. On one occasion, I lived in the home of a woman who had seven children and a very unsympathetic husband. She had lost two other children at birth. Though she had a large home to care for and attended to the family business in her spare time, I never saw her disturbed once. There was always the fragrance of Christ about her life, and I marveled at it.

While staying in her home during a conference, one morning about five o'clock I noticed light filtering in past the door; so I opened it very quietly and saw this woman kneeling by her piano. I quietly closed the door. The next morning the same thing happened, and the next morning the same thing again.

So, I asked her. "What time do you rise to seek the Lord?"

She replied, "Oh, that is not my decision. I made a

choice long ago that when He wanted to have fellowship with me I was available. There are times when He calls me at five; there are times when He calls at six. And on occasion, He will call about two o'clock in the morning, I think, just to test me."

Always she would get up, go to her piano stool, and worship her Lord.

I asked, "How long do you stay?"

"Oh, that is up to Him. When He tells me to go back to bed, I go back. If He doesn't want me to sleep, I simply stay up."

She was the epitome of serenity. She had made a choice, a choice that was not easy for her to make, for God had to take an idol out of her life before she made it; but when He took that idol, she was Christ's and Christ's alone.

Oh, yes, my dear sister, there is no excuse. With seven children she was busy, yes, but not troubled. That is the difference. You can be busy and not be troubled, or you cannot be busy and be very troubled. It all depends on whether Christ is central in your life.

We were created to worship Jesus Christ. We were created for Him, to become something to Him in order that He might find pleasure in us. But this demands discipline. This demands self-renunciation. This demands the mortifying of the flesh. This demands the taking out of our lives everything that does not contribute to the one great objective.

In John 11:20–22, we read of the death of Lazarus. The Lord Jesus arrives on the scene and is met by Martha.

> Now Martha, as soon as she heard that Jesus was
> coming, went and met him: but Mary was still sitting
> in the house. (v. 20)

Here you have again Martha the woman of action. "I must do something about this. I must go to the Lord."

> Now Martha said to Jesus, Lord, if You had been here,
> my brother would not have died. (v. 21)

Surely this is a tremendous attitude of faith toward the Lord; and these words were uttered by Martha, not Mary: "Lord, if You had been here, my brother would not have died."

What is she saying? "If You would have been present, You could have saved my brother from his illness. He would not have died." This is tremendous, and it is from Martha. Now she goes on to an even greater height of faith:

> "But even now I know that whatever You ask of God,
> God will give You." (v. 22).

"Even now," Martha says, "all is not lost."

Well, is that not wonderful? Has Martha, the busy woman with the complaining spirit, taken up with things, come to Mary's decision? I think not! For in verses 38 and 39 we read:

Then Jesus, again groaning in Himself, came to the tomb. It was a cave, and a stone lay against it. Jesus said, "Take away the stone."

Now the attitude of faith must become an act of faith. Next comes the test: "Take away the stone." Is the attitude of faith to be followed by the *act* of faith? Is the profession to be followed by the performance?

They are all gathered at the graveside. Only one person speaks. It is Martha. And what does she say in verse 39?

"Lord, by this time there is a stench, for he has been dead four days."

Where is her faith now? It is one thing to make a profession; it is quite a different thing to perform.

What does this reveal to us? Martha had an emotional spiritual experience because she had an inconsistent devotional life. Underline that, for this is always true of the person with an inconsistent devotional life. Today they are up in the heights, tomorrow down in the depths—an unstable, unreliable personality. "Lord, You can do anything; You can raise him from the dead." Then, "Oh no, Lord, he stinks. It can't be done."

Which are you? Martha or Mary? You must decide who you are to be. Have you ever chosen the one thing needful, the one thing that David chose? What was it? David chose to be occupied with the One he loved and to seek for Him with all his heart. Mary too chose the better part, and it was not taken from her.

Great was her reward, for we read in John 12:2–7:

> There they made Him a supper; and Martha served, but Lazarus was one of those who sat at the table with Him. Then Mary took a pound of very costly oil of spikenard, anointed the feet of Jesus, and wiped His feet with her hair. And the house was filled with the fragrance of the oil.
>
> But one of His disciples, Judas Iscariot, Simon's son, who would betray Him, said, "Why was this fragrant oil not sold for three hundred denarii, and given to the poor?" This he said, not that he cared for the poor, but because he was a thief, and had the money box; and he used to take what was put in it.
>
> But Jesus said, "Let her alone; she has kept this for the day of My burial."

What does this reveal to us? The person who makes the choice, who puts the one thing needful first, shares the innermost secrets of the heart of the Lord. It is that person to whom He will speak, for love demands a love of its kind.

The Lord Jesus loves us with all His heart. He desires that we love Him with all our heart; and until we do, we will never know the sweetness of His love for us. We will have some faint concept but that is all. With how many people do we share the secrets of our heart and with whom do we share them? We will be intimate with the person we know loves us, the person we know is committed to us, the person who has given himself or herself to us, and with none besides. It is so with our Lord. There must be the response of love to love.

Mary anointed Christ against His burial. How did she know? He revealed it to her. None of the others knew, but she knew. Why did He reveal it? Mary had chosen. She knew what it was to have intimate fellowship with her Lord; therefore, she received a great reward: the unspeakable honor of sharing the deep feelings of His heart.

Notes

1. Oswald Chambers, *My Utmost for His Highest* (New York: Dodd, Mead & Co., 1935), 254.
2. Carl F. Keil and Franz Delitzsch, *Psalms*, vol. 5 of Old Testament Commentaries (Grand Rapids: Eerdmans, 1978), 356–57.

Gracious God, we worship Thee,
Rev'rently we bow the knee;
Jesus Christ our only plea:
Father, we adore Thee.

∼

SAMUEL TREVOR FRANCIS

2

True Worship

The supreme thing is worship. The attitude of worship is the attitude of a subject bent before the King.
. . . The fundamental thought is that of prostration, of
bowing down. —G. CAMPBELL MORGAN

O ne time while I was ministering at a conference for
missionaries in the Philippine Islands a teenage
daughter of one of the missionaries came to me.

"Brother Carroll," she said, "I love my Lord. I never
miss my quiet time. I have a consistent prayer life, but
the Lord Jesus is not real to me. I want to love Him more
devotedly and serve Him more effectively, but I cannot
unless He becomes a reality to me. I read of the great
giants of the faith, how they were conscious of His presence; and I want that experience. Tell me, what shall I do?"

We chatted for a considerable time. A few days later I
met this young lady again.

"Mr. Carroll," she exclaimed, "for the first time in my
Christian life I am experiencing the conscious presence
of my Lord!"

A few years later, on a Monday evening after our
Bible class at the Evangelical Institute, I returned home rather tired and sat down
to relax, only to be interrupted by
my wife calling that deadly word,
"Telephone."

"Who is it?"

"I don't know, but he says that he is a preacher in Chicago. He is rather excited. He says you changed his life."

I answered the call.

"Are you Brother Carroll?"

"Yes."

"You have changed my life."

"Well, I hope the Lord did it."

"No, no, of course the Lord did it; but it was those messages."

"Which messages?"

"Those tapes on worship. They have changed my life." What changed his life? Jesus Christ had become a reality to him.

Is He that to you? Do you walk with Him and know Him? Is He a reality?

Reality through Worship

A few years after that missions conference in the Philippines and the phone call from the Chicago pastor, I was invited to a Midwestern city for a series of meetings. During the final gathering, which was for pastors, I spoke very simply on the same message that I had shared with the teenager in the Philippines and that pastor in Chicago. When I returned to that city a year later, I was met by one of the pastors.

"Do you recall the message you gave a year ago?" he asked.

"Yes."

"Well, since then my church has had a new pastor;

and I have had a new congregation."

What was the message I gave to those preachers, to the Chicago pastor, and to the young lady in the Philippines? It was a simple message on worship, the worship of Jesus Christ.

What would you say? What would your answer be if someone asked, "What is the blessing derived from worshiping God?" The experience of one of the great defenders of the faith, C. S. Lewis, helps us to answer the question. He writes about the experience that led to his discovery of the primacy of worship:

> When I first began to draw near to belief in God and even for some time after it had been given to me, I found a stumbling block in the demand so clamorously made by all religious people that we should "praise" God; still more in the suggestion that God Himself demanded it. We all despise the man who demands continued assurance of his own virtue, intelligence or delightfulness; we despise still more the crowd of people round every dictator, every millionaire, every celebrity who gratify that demand. Thus a picture, at once ludicrous and horrible, both of God and of His worshippers, threatened to appear in my mind. The Psalms were especially troublesome in this way— "Praise the Lord," "O praise the Lord with me," "Praise Him." . . . It was hideously like saying, "What I most want is to be told that I am good and great." . . . And mere quantity of praise seemed to count; "seven times a day do I praise thee" (119:164 KJV). It was extremely

distressing. It made one think what one least wanted
to think. Gratitude to God, reverence to Him, obedience to Him, I thought I could understand; not
this perpetual eulogy. Nor were matters mended by
a modern author who talked of God's "right" to be
praised.[1]

So here was his dilemma. Lewis was a young Christian
searching with an open, honest heart, yet this matter of
praise was becoming a great stumbling block. Why does
God want to be praised and eulogized? Why does He
always want to be the center of affection and attention?

Then he got his answer: "I did not see *that it is in the
process of being worshipped that God communicates His
presence to men. . . .* Even in Judaism the essence of the
sacrifice was not really that men gave bulls and goats
to God, but that by their so doing God gave Himself to
men"[2] (italics added).

In other words, it was in that act of worship that He
became a reality to them.

What a wonderful discovery for Lewis to make so
early in his Christian experience. Note carefully his important statement: "It is in the process of being worshipped that God communicates His presence to men."

What Is True Worship?

What then is worship? The term comes to us in our
modern speech from the Anglo-Saxon "weorth-scipe,"
which later developed into "worship," meaning "to attribute worth to an object." Worship is the "worthship" of

the one you worship. To worship Jesus Christ is to attribute worth to Him.

As Revelation is, above all other books, the key to worship of Jesus Christ, we must consider Revelation 4:10–11:

> The twenty-four elders fall down before Him who sits on the throne and worship him who lives forever and ever, and cast their crowns before the throne, saying: "You are worthy, O Lord, to receive glory and honor and power; for You created all things, and by Your will they exist and were created."

Here is true worship, and the order is significant. The first thing in verse 10 is that the twenty-four fall down "before Him who sits on the throne." That is first, and that is always first. The falling down speaks of submission to the One worshiped, for here we find that they "fall down . . . and worship Him who lives forever and ever, and cast their crowns before the throne." It is imperative that we observe that there is first the submission and second the casting of their crowns before the throne.

In the days when Revelation was written, when a king was conquered by the Roman legions, either he was brought to Rome to prostrate himself at the emperor's feet or a massive image of Caesar was placed before him, and he was required to fall down, casting his crown at its feet. This was his act of total submission, of abdication to the emperor. So John the apostle, in Revelation 4, is revealing the first two essentials of worship. The first is the falling down, the submission to the One worshiped. The second is the casting of the crown at the feet of the One worshiped.

Now, what is the purpose of the crown? It is to draw attention to the one wearing it. It exalts the wearer. The true worshiper of Christ, in casting his crown at his Lord's feet, is saying, "I want You alone to be exalted, You alone to be glorified." The second requirement, then, is the desire to live for the glory of Christ and Christ alone.

The first essential condition for true worship is total submission. The second essential is that Christ alone should be glorified. We must meet these conditions, submitting ourselves absolutely, without reserve, to Jesus Christ as Lord.

In Revelation 4:11, we find the worshipers ascribing worth to the One on the throne, telling Him that He is worthy. This is worship: the "worthship" of the one worshiped.

> You are worthy, O Lord, to receive glory and honor and power; for You created all things, and by Your will they exist and were created.

What have they done? They have abdicated and cast their crowns before the throne, divesting themselves of their glory and saying, "You are worthy to receive glory, and You alone." Honor and power follow. These three things are what men seek: to be glorified, to be exalted, to be honored. Therefore, to worship Jesus Christ we must divest ourselves of all desire for glory and honor and power; for He and He alone is worthy of such.

Revelation 5 is one of the great chapters, if not the greatest chapter, on worship in all the Bible. Notice again the order in verse 8: first they fall down.

> Now when He had taken the scroll, the four living creatures and the twenty-four elders fell down before the Lamb, each having a harp, and golden bowls of incense, which are the prayers of the saints.

Again in verse 9, they are ascribing worth to Jesus Christ. This is worship.

> And they sang a new song, saying: "You are worthy to take the scroll, and to open its seals; for You were slain, and have redeemed us to God by Your blood out of every tribe and tongue and people and nation.

Obviously, then, we cannot worship unless there is total submission of our hearts.

> All the angels stood around the throne and the elders and the four living creatures, and fell on their faces before the throne and worshiped God. (Revelation 7:11)

Difficulties in Worship

Worship is not simple, but it is glorious! I have found these many years that it is the one thing the Enemy will oppose more than anything else—more than intercession, more than petition. The one thing he does not want is for you to worship Jesus Christ.

Developing Spiritual Senses

Worship is not simple because the rewards are so great. As we learn to give ourselves to the worship of our Lord, He can be nearer and more real to us than our best friend or closest loved one. The rewards are indeed great, but the amazing fact is that very few worship Jesus Christ. Therefore, their spiritual senses are not quickened to His presence.

We know that the body has senses; but the spirit also has senses, and it is by the senses of our spirit that we are made conscious of the presence of Christ. "God is a Spirit" who can only be worshiped by that which is spiritual in us, by our spirits. To many this is difficult because we cannot see Him with our physical eyes or touch Him with our physical hands, but He can be seen and touched and handled by the senses of our spirits.

Setting the Will

It is not a matter of saying, "I see this truth, and I do want to be a worshiper." No, for we are not what we wish to be or want to be, but what we will to be. You must therefore set your will to become a worshiper of Christ. You will never be a worshiper of Christ apart from a definite act of your will.

When you first begin to worship, you may ascribe worth to Him only to conclude, "Well, I don't know. I did it all but nothing happened." You must persevere.

There was a man in Detroit, a valiant Christian, who when trapped in a hotel fire was badly burned and brought almost to the point of death. Upon recovery and discovering that he was blind, his one lament was that he could no longer read his Bible; so he requested that he be taught Braille. When the tips of his fingers, so badly burned and now scarred, were tested, there was no sensitivity in them. His toes, his lips, and finally his tongue were tested; and with his tongue he read the Bible through three times!

Senses are quickened by use.

Having experienced the conscious presence of Christ in worship, we must be careful to obey the inward promptings of the Holy Spirit when He calls us to worship. When under severe pressure I have been tempted to turn aside from the essential of worship, I have suffered loss in many areas of my Christian experience. Always there had to be the determination to come back and give myself again to worship of the Lamb on the throne.

Maintaining Priorities

In the temptation of our Lord in the wilderness, we are introduced to the subtle attempt of the Enemy to bring our Lord under his control.

> Again, the devil took Him up on an exceedingly high mountain, and showed Him all the kingdoms of the world and their glory. And he said to Him, "All these things I will give You if You will fall down and worship me." (Matthew 4:8–9)

Notice that Satan has the correct order. He says, "I will give You all the kingdoms and the glory of them. All I want is for You to fall down and worship me. That is all I want."

Very clever! . . . for you will serve the one you worship. What is the use of having the kingdoms of the world and the glory of them if Satan has you? The Lord would have the kingdoms, but Satan would have Him. The person you truly worship will control you. Even the man in the world knows this. Have you not heard people say, "She worships her husband," "He worships his wife," or, "They worship their son"? Such persons are saying that they live for the one they worship. You will serve the one you worship. You will not have to be motivated or forced.

The importance of our Lord's revealing statement "You shall worship the Lord your God, and Him only you shall serve" (v. 10), is seen in its order: worship first, then service. Worship always precedes service.

Then observe "Him only you shall serve."

"But," you might say, "I serve my church."

No, you primarily serve the Lord in your church. You may be dissatisfied with certain things happening in your church; you cannot be dissatisfied with the Lord. He has placed you there to serve Him.

For ten years I had the privilege of ministering to groups of missionaries in the Orient on some very difficult fields. Often in the first term, the missionary comes up against formidable obstacles.

For instance, the Devil might say to him concerning

the nationals, "These people are deceitful. They are not worth serving. You cannot lay down your life for such."

Oh, but you are laying down your life for the nationals as a service to Jesus Christ. Do you see the difference?

Did not the apostle Paul describe himself and his co-workers as "your servants for Jesus' sake"? The true missionary is held by a Person, Jesus, who alone can sustain him and hold him in the fire (and a missionary is in the fire often). Nothing else will suffice. The missionary can give up, or lose the will to fight, or go home. But if he or she knows the Lord Jesus intimately and what it is to worship Him and serve Him, the missionary will not be defeated.

The more we worship our Lord, loving Him, serving Him, and expressing that love for Him in serving others as His willing slaves, the more we will desire to worship and serve Him.

One of the keys to effective service is found in 2 Corinthians 3:17–18 (KJV), where we read:

Now the Lord is that Spirit: and where the Spirit of the Lord is, there is liberty. But we all, with open face beholding as in a glass the glory of the Lord, are changed into the same image from glory to glory, even as by the Spirit of the Lord.

This is what Hudson Taylor called "changed by beholding." Changed into what? Changed into the same image of the One worshiped or made Christlike. How simple. Yet, how glorious!

It is the desire of the Spirit of God that we behold Jesus, that we be taken up with Him, that we worship Him; and as we worship Him, what is happening? The Spirit of God is making us like the One we worship.

Anyone with a knowledge of missions knows that the person in a pagan land looks before she listens. She wants to see something different. And does she not have a right to see Christ in a missionary? If the missionary is a worshiper of Jesus Christ, she will.

An outstanding Christian in Japan today is a medical doctor who saw a missionary in whom she could not deny that Christ dwelt. This encounter was the beginning of her thirst to know Christ.

One of the most esteemed missions in the world is Dohnavur in South India. The founder of that mission, Amy Carmichael, was admired by all who knew her for her determination to always seek God's "pattern in the mount" for anything that took place at Dohnavur.

When a large chapel was needed, after much prayer she determined that it would be placed in the very center of the mission compound. It was to have two spires. How unusual! One spire, yes. Two spires, why? The Lord had a reason for this. The spire at the front of the chapel was to represent worship. The spire at the rear was to represent service. Whenever those spires were seen during the day, all were reminded that worship must precede service.

Amy Carmichael herself labored for forty years without a furlough. Little wonder that God has so signally blessed the literature from Dohnavur.

You will recall that famous incident that took place

in the experience of Isaiah. We are told that in the year that King Uzziah died he "saw the Lord sitting on a throne, high and lifted up" (Isaiah 6:1). He also saw seraphim worshiping the Lord. Each one had six wings: two to cover his face, two to cover his feet, and two to fly, to carry out the will of the One worshiped. I wonder why he did not fly with six? If you gave most Christians today six wings, what would they want to do? Go as fast as they could! But where?

Oh, no, four are to prepare for worship; only two are for service.

The worship of the One on the throne by the seraphim prepared them for swift, obedient service. It is always the same order: worship before service.

Notes

1. C. S. Lewis, *Reflections on the Psalms* (New York: Harcourt, Brace, Jovanovich, 1958), 90–91.

2. Ibid., 93.

I thank Thee, uncreated Sun,
That thy bright beams on me have shined;
I thank Thee, who hast overthrown
My foes, and healed my wounded mind;
I thank Thee, whose enlivening voice
Bids my freed heart in Thee rejoice.

JOHN WESLEY

3

A True Heart

There must be the inward worship within the shrine
if there is to be outward service. —ALEXANDER
MCLAREN

During my first visit to Japan I was invited to speak at a conference that was quite close to Mt. Fuji. I had heard a great deal about Mt. Fuji and was looking forward to seeing this mighty mountain the Japanese worship. As we were making our way to the conference grounds, the director of the mission spoke to me about Fuji.

"From our conference grounds you have possibly the best view of the mountain in the country, and the time to behold Fuji is early in the morning. Be up early, and you will get an excellent view."

There was a heavy mist when we arrived, so we could not even think of seeing anything of Fuji that afternoon. But the director assured me, "Be up early in the morning, and you will see Fuji in all its beauty."

So I was up very early the next morning; and looking out the window, all I could see was mist. All that day the mist overshadowed the conference ground. There was no sign of Fuji. The mountain was there, but I could not behold it.

The second morning I was up early again—still mist. So I said to my friend Rollie Reasoner, "Rollie, do you think this mist will evaporate? Do you think I will ever see the mountain?"

"Now be patient; be patient, Joe. Possibly tomorrow."

The next morning, again nothing but mist. I had almost given up when on the last morning of the conference I arose, this time not so early, looked out my window and saw magnificent, conical shaped, snow-capped Fuji; and as I gazed, transfixed, I realized why the Japanese worship this mountain.

Heart Worship

Fuji was always there; but I could not see the great sight, for the mist had to be taken away. God is always present when we worship Him; but you can desire to see Him in His glory and His beauty and His wonder, and never do so. Why? If there is a mist, the mist of an unsurrendered heart, there can be no acceptable approach to Him.

A certain princess once went to visit her grandmother, who was a very regal woman. She dashed into her grandmother's presence and jumped up onto her lap.

Grandmother promptly dumped her on the floor and said, "Now come in as a princess should."

So the chastened princess came in, curtsied, and requested permission to sit on Grandmother's lap.

There is an acceptable approach to God. What is it? We read in Hebrews 10:22: "Let us draw near with a true heart."

Drawing near with a true heart is the first condition of acceptable approach to God for true worship. We can honor God with our lips, but we worship Him with our heart. True worship is heart worship.

In Matthew 15:7–8, our Lord in a clear manner revealed why those in Isaiah's day were hypocrites or play actors: "Hypocrites! Well did Isaiah prophesy about you, saying: 'These people draw near to Me with their mouth, and honor Me with their lips, but their heart is far from Me.'"

What an indictment! What did they have? They had confession without commitment. There must be commitment, the commitment of a true heart, for acceptable worship.

What Is the Heart?

When Scripture speaks about the heart, what is it saying to us? Let us consider the first three references to the heart in Scripture.

> The Lord saw that the wickedness of man was great in the earth, and that every intent of the thoughts of his heart was only evil continually. (Genesis 6:5)

When we are speaking about the heart we are speaking about the intellect: "the thoughts of his heart."

> And the Lord was sorry that He had made man on the earth, and He was grieved in His heart. (Genesis 6:6)

When we are speaking about the heart in Scripture, we are speaking about the intellect and also about the emotions, for grief is an emotion.

> And the Lord smelled a soothing aroma. Then the
> Lord said in His heart, "I will never again curse the
> ground for man's sake." (Genesis 8:21)

God, the Lord, said in His heart, "I will not." In other words, the heart is that center within us where three things are perpetually being oriented: the intellect, the emotion, and the will. Handley Moule, the great evangelical scholar, has this to say about the heart: "It is the organ of personality" (that is, the intellect, emotion, and will).

What Is a True Heart?

We know what the heart is from Scripture, but what is a *true* heart? Unless we understand this condition and meet it, we cannot acceptably approach God; and we will not experience true worship. I am not saying that we cannot come into the presence of God. We can, but we cannot worship in the way God desires us to worship. We will go through the motions, but that is all. We have seen quite clearly from the Word of God that the first thing in worship is the prostration, the falling down. This is submission. There must be a true heart of submission when we come to God in worship; otherwise, our worship is unacceptable.

Bishop Westcott, who wrote a classic on the epistle to the Hebrews, said that a true heart is "a heart which expresses completely the devotion of the whole person to God. There is no divided allegiance, no reserve of feeling."[1]

This is perfect self-surrender of the whole person; in other words, it is the intellect, the emotion, and the will.

Another scholar who has given us a classic on Hebrews is Adolph Saphir. He has this to say: "What is meant by a true heart? . . . Only a whole heart is true. . . . A true heart is never pleased with itself; but it is at peace, content that Jesus shall be all."[2]

Andrew Murray, who has given us possibly the best devotional classic on Hebrews, has this to say about a true heart: "In man's nature the heart is the central power. As the heart is so is the man. . . Our inmost being must in truth be yielded to Him. . . . It is only as the desire of the heart is fixed upon God, the whole heart seeking for God, giving its love and finding its joy in God, that a man can draw nigh to God."[3]

This may possibly cause you to think, "What hope do I have for a true heart? Can I fix the desire of my heart upon God? Can my whole heart seek for God, giving its love to and finding its joy in God? Can I do that?"

If you seek for a true heart with all your heart, you will receive it. It is entirely your decision, for God's callings are His enablings. He lives in you by His Spirit to meet His own demands. Most certainly, without the enabling Spirit, such a heart is impossible; but with the Spirit controlling, it is the very life into which He will lead you.

Abraham's Surrender

In Genesis 22:1–2, we read of the great surrender of Abraham. Let us therefore note carefully what he surrenders.

Now it came to pass after these things that God tested Abraham, and said to him, "Abraham!" And he said, "Here I am."

Then He said, "Take now your son, your only son Isaac, whom you love, and go to the land of Moriah, and offer him there as a burnt offering on one of the mountains of which I shall tell you."

What is He saying to Abraham? "You must put Isaac to death. You must offer him as a burnt offering. Your only son whom you love, you must place on an altar." What a test! But we would do well to remember that when God tests a person it is because He wants to bless him. This test is going to be severe; but if Abraham passes it, the blessing is to be not only for him but also for multitudes.

His Heart

Now before Abraham can obey, he is going to have to surrender three things. The first thing is his intellect. What God has asked him to do does not make sense. It defies the understanding. Why? Isaac is the child of promise. He is the miracle child. All depends upon Isaac. Now God says to put him to death. Well, God will raise him up; but why put him to death if He is going to raise him up? It makes no sense.

Therefore, the first thing Abraham must surrender is his intellect. Abraham had to yield to the imperative of Proverbs 3:5: "Trust in the Lord with all your heart, and lean not on your own understanding."

This is a command of God. It is a command we need before us during these days when we are apt to lean on our own understanding, apt to lean on what man can do by his trained intellect, apt to become the victims of a subtle, man-centered, religious humanism. The intellect must be surrendered. This is the first thing.

What must he surrender next? Abraham must surrender his affections, his emotions. He loved Isaac, so he must surrender his emotions.

And, finally, he must surrender his will. He must will to do the will of God in preference to his own will.

In other words, what is God asking Abraham to do? He is asking him to surrender his heart—his intellect, his emotion, and his will—that he might do the will of God. This is the test. This is also the test for us, for it means death to what we want in order that we might have what God wants.

Surely if there was one thing that Abraham wanted, it was that Isaac be preserved. Offer his son, his only son whom he loved? Anything but that! But what did Abraham do? Did he call his friends together and say, "Now we must have a prayer meeting. I must seek the Lord about a big decision that I must make."

Oh, no! "Abraham rose early in the morning" (Genesis 22:3). He rose in immediate, unquestioning, un-hesitating obedience to the revealed will of God. When God speaks, we do not have to pray. We can ask for grace, that is true; but we do not have to seek guidance.

When did you surrender your heart to the Lord? Surrender of the intellect and emotions apart from the will is no surrender. When did you yield yourself in totality to the Lord? Do you have a true heart? That is what God wants, and that is what He must have. That is the great imperative.

His Service

> So Abraham rose early in the morning and saddled his
> donkey, and took two of his young men with him, and
> Isaac his son; and he split the wood for the burnt of-
> fering, and arose and went to the place of which God
> had told him. Then on the third day Abraham lifted
> his eyes and saw the place afar off. And Abraham said
> to his young men, "Stay here with the donkey; the lad
> and I will go yonder and worship, and we will come
> back to you." (vv. 3–5)

Notice three things that should characterize all service. Abraham went in obedience to the revealed will of God. We do not choose our own service. God reveals to us what He desires us to do by His Spirit; and the response must be unquestioning, unhesitating obedience. Next we will notice that he went to worship; and, finally, he went in faith. We see three things: he went in obedience, he went to worship, he went in faith: "The lad and I will go yonder and worship, and we will come back to you." He is going to offer him up. Yes, but he believes God will raise him from the dead because God is true to His Word.

What faith! Do we believe God's Word like that? Do we believe that what He says is true even if it takes a miracle?

His Altar

> So Abraham took the wood of the burnt offering and laid it on Isaac his son; and he took the fire in his hand, and a knife; and the two of them went together. But Isaac spoke to Abraham his father and said, "My father!" And he said, "Here am I, my son."
>
> Then he said, "Look, the fire and the wood, but where is the lamb for a burnt offering?"
>
> And Abraham said, "My son, God will provide for Himself the lamb for a burnt offering." So the two of them went together.
>
> Then they came to the place of which God had told him. And Abraham built an altar there and placed the wood in order; and he bound Isaac his son and laid him on the altar, upon the wood. (Genesis 22:6–9)

They came to the place of which God had told him, and Abraham built an altar. He may have built it with trembling hands, with tears streaming down his cheeks; but he built it. Before we can acceptably worship God, we have to do the same thing. We will have to build an altar with our own hands, with the hands of our heart; but we are not going to lay Isaac on that altar. We are going to lay ourselves on that altar to be a burnt offering, wholly consumed for the glory of God. Abraham built an altar; and when he had completed it, he laid the one he loved, his only son, upon that altar.

> And Abraham stretched out his hand and took the knife to slay his son. (v. 10)

The moment has arrived. The altar has been built and the offering has been bound. Now he raises the knife. What happens?

> But the Angel of the Lord called to him from heaven and said, "Abraham, Abraham!"
>
> So he said, "Here I am."
>
> And He said, "Do not lay your hand on the lad, or do anything to him; for now I know that you fear God, since you have not withheld your son, your only son, from Me."
>
> Then Abraham lifted his eyes and looked, and there behind him was a ram caught in a thicket by his horns. So Abraham went and took the ram, and offered it up for a burnt offering instead of his son. And Abraham called the name of that place, The-Lord-Will-Provide; as it is said to this day, "In the Mount of the Lord it shall be provided."
>
> Then the Angel of the Lord called to Abraham a second time out of heaven, and said: "By myself I have sworn, says the Lord, because you have done this thing, and have not withheld your son, your only son—blessing I will bless you, and multiplying I will multiply your descendants as the stars of the heaven and as the sand which is on the seashore; and your descendants shall possess the gate of their enemies. In your seed all the nations of the earth shall be blessed; because you have obeyed My voice." (vv. 11–18)

"By myself I have sworn, says the Lord, for because you have done this thing." "This thing"? What did he do? He surrendered his heart. Abraham had done many things. He had left his home. He had left his kindred. He had become a wanderer on the face of the earth. He had become a tent dweller. He had done many things, but all of those past surrenders were leading to this great surrender. Now is the test, the great test. "Because you have done this thing . . . in your seed all the nations of the earth shall be blessed."

What a blessing! Here is one man with a true heart, and all the nations of the earth are blessed through him!

Surrendered Servants

While I was in South America for a conference, a mission leader shared with me that he had spoken to the president of a well-known Bible college and said, "You are not giving us the missionaries that once came from your Bible college."

The president had a simple answer: "I am not receiving the same quality of students."

Why? It is because we have diluted God's requirement. We have majored in statistics (which is a secular concept), whereas God requires a whole heart; for no man can be filled with the Spirit or worship God acceptably unless he has such a heart. But let that man yield to the Spirit of God as He works within him to bring him to that place of a true heart, and God can bless a multitude through him.

Here are five examples of those who offered a true

heart, wholly surrendered to God.

D. L. Moody

What was the key to the life of D. L. Moody? He once heard British evangelist Henry Varley say, "The world has yet to see what God can do through a man wholly consecrated to Him."[4]

D. L. Moody said, "By the grace of God, I will be that man."

We all know how God used D. L. Moody. Was it because he was brilliant, because he was gifted, because he was educated, because he was a man of essentially superlative gifts? No, he was a man with a perfect heart who proved the truth of 2 Chronicles 16:9: "For the eyes of the Lord run to and fro throughout the whole earth, to show Himself strong on behalf of those whose heart is loyal to Him."

It is not what we can do for God; it is what God will do for us and through us when we have a perfect heart. He is waiting for such men; He is waiting for such women; and when God finds such a man or such a woman, He will show Himself strong in their behalf. We must never forget that it is not what we can do for God; it is what He waits to do for us and through us that glorifies Him.

We must perfect our hearts. There must be that altar in our lives upon which we have laid our intellect, emotion, and will to be God's man, God's woman, if God is to use us as His tried and trusted servants.

Graham Scroggie

I was present at the famous Keswick Convention in England in the early 1950s when the Bible readings were given by Graham Scroggie. A master expositor, he delivered his message with great power. But more than the message was the man himself: his intensity, his obvious love for Christ, his masterly grasp of the Scriptures. The consciousness of the Spirit of God speaking through the man is what impressed me.

At the conclusion of his first message, he gave a word of personal testimony. On one occasion while ministering, he was suddenly taken with illness. The illness persisted, and he consulted his doctor concerning what he should do. A diagnosis was made, and the doctor informed him that the only cure would be for him to cease from preaching; for if he continued preaching, there was no cure. In his dilemma Scroggie cried to the Lord and was led to seek counsel from Grattan Guinness, a close and trusted friend in Ireland.

Back from his friend came a Spirit-directed, unusual letter. "Scroggie," he said, "have you ever truly surrendered to Jesus Christ?" What a question to ask a famous preacher, but it is a very important question to ask anybody.

Scroggie replied, "I have in a general sort of way."

Back came another letter from his friend. "Do it in a deliberate, specific manner."

Again, Scroggie sought the Lord; and in the stillness of His presence powerful conviction gripped him. He realized that he had been living for his preaching, living to make a name as a preacher; and it had grieved his Lord. So in tears, he yielded himself in a deliberate, specific manner to be God's man, not Scroggie's, and was healed, going on to preach for many years with great power.

When did you surrender to Jesus Christ? You might give the same answer as Dr. Scroggie, "Well, I have surrendered in a general sort of a way." Well, do it in a deliberate, specific manner; and do it once for all. You must give up your right to yourself. Intellect, emotion, and will must be yielded in a deliberate, specific manner.

F. B. Meyer

F. B. Meyer, another of the great Bible teachers of his day, was mightily used not only in England but also throughout the world. He was greatly gifted and had a brilliant mind.

As a young man with a thriving reputation, he went to a farewell meeting for a number of graduates of Cambridge University who were going out to China. These young men were called the Cambridge Seven. One of them was a young man named Charlie Studd, the most famous sportsman in England, for the captain of the English cricket team was always considered the foremost athlete in the land. Now he was turning his back upon the world of sport to go to China with the China Inland Mission.

That afternoon as he gave his testimony, F. B. Meyer listened intently. It was not so much what F. B. Meyer heard, as what he saw and felt; for it was obvious that C. T. Studd was a man totally yielded to Jesus Christ.

A statement that C. T. Studd once made perhaps sums up the whole man: "If Jesus Christ be God and died for me, then no sacrifice can be too great for me to make for Him."[5]

After the meeting F. B. Meyer went to Charlie Studd and said, "It is quite obvious that you have something that I lack, something that I need. What is it?"

C. T. Studd in his very forthright manner looked him straight in the eye and asked, "Have you ever surrendered everything to Jesus Christ?"

F. B. Meyer thought a moment and said, "Yes, I have."

But a small voice within said, "No, you have not."

Deeply troubled, he made his way home, hurried to his bedroom, fell to his knees, and began to pray. He tells us that when he was praying it seemed as if the Lord came to him and said, "Meyer, I want all the keys to your heart."

F. B. Meyer began to argue a little with the Lord. "All the keys?"

"Yes, Meyer, I want all the keys."

Then F. B. Meyer deceitfully took a ring of keys and handed them over to the Lord. But you cannot fool the Lord. There was one missing. The Lord, it seemed, F. B. Meyer tells us, took that ring of keys and began to count them carefully. When He had finished, the Lord looked at him and said, "There is one key missing; and if I am not Lord of all, I am not Lord at all." Then, He turned as if He would leave the room.

In his dilemma, F. B. Meyer cried out to Him, "Lord, don't leave! Why are you leaving?"

Back came the word, "If I am not Lord of all, I am not Lord at all."[6]

"But Lord, it's just a very small key, a very small place in my heart."

Back again came the word, "If I am not Lord of all, I am not Lord at all."

In desperation, F. B. Meyer surrendered that last key. And what happened? He became a Spirit-controlled man who was a blessing to countless multitudes. Even today his magnificent books speak in many languages.

That was the crisis of his life. He had to build an altar, and he had to place F. B. Meyer upon the altar. Every key had to be surrendered.

Archibald Brown

In the days of C. H. Spurgeon there were other famous preachers, and one of them was a man named Archibald Brown. He was a gifted preacher but not a great preacher until the Spirit of God began to work in his heart; then certain things began to take place in his life. One evening, up in his study, Archibald Brown was rather disturbed, for God was speaking to him. He was so disturbed that upon reaching the top of the stairs he suddenly tripped and fell. When he had recovered himself at the bottom of the stairs, realizing that God had spoken to him, he cried, "Lord, anything!"

Back came the word, "Not anything, *everything*." That is what changed Archibald Brown from just another good preacher to a great preacher.

Not all are called to be preachers, but we all need

a true heart to worship God; for worship is the highest art of which a man or woman is capable in the spiritual realm and the imperative preparation for any service.

Nicolaus von Zinzendorf

In these days we are all conscious, I believe, of the desperate need for revival. If you are a student of revival, you will know that possibly the purest of all revivals was that which took place among the Moravians in 1727 under the leadership of Count von Zinzendorf.[7] And what was the key to that great movement of God? The key was the worship of the slain Lamb.

As a young man, Count von Zinzendorf visited an art gallery in Germany. Admiring the various, priceless paintings, he was suddenly transfixed by one. As the curator of the art gallery made his rounds, he noticed this young man gazing intently at that painting hour after hour. Finally when it came time to close the gallery, the young Count was still there. At last the curator went to him and put his hand on his shoulder. He was about to tell him that he must leave when he saw tears streaming down the young man's cheeks. There in front of von Zinzendorf was a magnified painting of the slain Lamb of God, beneath which were the words, "All this I did for thee. What hast thou done for Me?" Before that painting of the crucified Christ, the Holy Spirit spoke; and Nicolaus von Zinzendorf from that day had a broken heart.

What is a true heart? It is a heart that is broken, broken from self, and offered up to God.

NOTES

1. B. F. Westcott, *The Epistle to the Hebrews* (reprint, Grand Rapids: Eerdmans, 1977), 322.

2. Adolph Saphir, *The Epistle to the Hebrews* (New York: Loizeaux Brothers, n.d.), 665–66.

3. Andrew Murray, *The Holiest of All* (Old Tappan, N.J.: Fleming H. Revell, n.d.), 369.

4. *More Than 2,000 Great Quotes and Illustrations*, comp. George Sweeting (Dallas: Word, 1985), 142; cf. 85.

5. Norman Grubb, *C. T. Studd, Cricketer & Pioneer* (Ft. Washington, PA: Christian Literature Crusade, 1982), 132.

6. Ibid., 46.

7. A. Kenneth Curtis, "A Golden Summer: The Moravian Renewal of 1727," November 2011, http://www. zinzendorf.com.

*Oh, worship the Lord in the
beauty of holiness,
Bow down before Him, His glory
proclaim; With gold of obedience,
and incense of lowliness,
Kneel and adore Him;
the Lord is His name.*

~

JOHN MONSELL

Revelation 4 and 5

Revelation and worship are the foundation of everything. —W. H. GRIFFITH THOMAS

An understanding of Revelation 4 and 5 is essential as
an aid to true worship of the Lord, for in these two
chapters we have a glimpse into heaven. First, in chapter
4 we see the One who sits on the throne; then in chapter
5 we behold the Lamb.

Exposition of Revelation 4

Vision of God

> After these things I looked, and behold, a door stand-
> ing open in heaven. And the first voice which I heard
> was like a trumpet speaking with me, saying, "Come
> up here, and I will show you things which must take
> place after this."
>
> Immediately I was in the Spirit; and behold, a
> throne set in heaven, and One sat on the throne. And
> He who sat there was like a jasper and a
> sardius stone in appearance; and there
> was a rainbow around the throne,
> in appearance like an emerald.
> (Revelation 4:1–3)

In the first verse, John is commanded by the voice like a trumpet, the voice of our Lord Himself, to "come up here" to see things that will take place. Then John "immediately . . . in the Spirit" beheld "a throne set in heaven, and One [who] sat on the throne."

John then attempts to describe the glory and the majesty of the One who sits on the throne, God Himself. So he says in verse 3, "He who sat there was like a jasper and a sardius stone in appearance." We can be assured that the jasper was as clear as crystal, a diamond. A sardius, or a cornelian stone, as it could be translated, was possibly a ruby; but it was a red stone. These two together speak of the glory and the sacrifice of God.

Then John tells us there was "a rainbow around about the throne, in appearance like an emerald." The rainbow here speaks of the covenant-keeping God. It signifies that God is faithful, that God keeps His covenant. The rainbow that followed the great flood was a symbol that God is faithful and is a God of mercy. It is instructive and wonderful to know that this rainbow round about the throne was likened to an emerald; for an emerald, the color green, always speaks of mercy.

So here we have this wonderful Being, this wonderful Person on the throne who is merciful. John, in trying to describe Him, speaks of the glory, the sacrifice, the mercy, and the faithfulness of this One who sits on the throne.

Vision of the Throne

Around the throne were twenty-four thrones, and on the thrones I saw twenty-four elders sitting, clothed

in white robes; and they had crowns of gold on their
heads. And from the throne proceeded lightnings,
thunderings, and voices. Seven lamps of fire were
burning before the throne, which are the seven Spirits
of God.

Before the throne there was a sea of glass, like
crystal. And in the midst of the throne, and around
the throne, were four living creatures full of eyes in
front and in back. The first living creature was like a
lion, the second living creature like a calf, the third
living creature had a face like a man, and the fourth
living creature was like a flying eagle. The four living
creatures, each having six wings, were full of eyes
around and within. And they do not rest day or night,
saying: "Holy, holy, holy, Lord God Almighty, who
was and is and is to come!" (4:4–8)

In verse 4, we have the central throne, and around
the throne are these twenty-four thrones occupied by
the twenty-four elders. There are differing opinions
as to who these elders are, but I believe we can be assured that they are representative of all believers. Now
a throne speaks of authority, of power, of rulership, or
prominence. Not only are the twenty-four elders seated
upon these thrones, but they have crowns on their heads.
A crown speaks of victory. They are victors. So the picture here is quite clear. In the center is the throne of God,
and round the throne are twenty-four thrones. Seated on
these twenty-four thrones are the elders, representative
of the believers of all times.

Then in verse 5 we read, "And from the throne proceeded lightnings, thunderings, and voices. Seven lamps of fire were burning before the throne, which are the seven Spirits of God." Notice here that the Spirit of God is described under the emblem of fire, the fire of the Spirit that burns against all sin; this speaks of the sevenfold plenitude of the Spirit's power. So, we have the lamps of fire, the thunderings, and the voices in the center surrounded by these thrones.

This fifth verse can also remind us that God is a covenant-keeping God. The rainbow recalls the covenant with Noah. The flaming torches refer us to the covenant with Abraham. The thunderings and lightnings can be associated with the covenant at Sinai.[1]

Then we are introduced to a sea in verse 6: "Before the throne there was a sea of glass, like crystal. And in the midst of the throne, and around the throne, were four living creatures full of eyes in front and in back." The "sea like as of glass" is a better rendering, and it speaks of the Word of God. Later we read of the martyrs standing on this sea like unto crystal. It is a great sea. This great, vast sea is before the throne and reveals to us, or speaks to us, not only of the eternal character and purity of the Word of God but also of the distance that is always between the worshiper and God Himself.

Now, in our modern day we are apt to have an unholy familiarity with God, an attitude we will never have if we have an understanding of the book of Revelation. To some He is simply a Person who exists in order that He might save people on their terms and help them live the life they want to live; and when they are in trouble, He will help them out. This concept of God is not like the God of the Bible. He is the great God of the universe who gave His Son to be a propitiation for our sin, not that we might live a life that pleases us but that we might live a life that pleases Him. This great One upon the throne with the vast sea before Him, He is the God of Glory.

Then in verses 6–8 we read of "four living creatures . . . each having six wings, [and] were full of eyes around and within. And they do not rest day or night, saying: "Holy, holy, holy, Lord God Almighty, who was and is and is to come!"

These four creatures represent all that is mightiest and grandest in creation. The six wings and the eyes speak of incessant activity.

Worship of God

Then we come to that passage we have already referred to, a passage of vast importance:

> Whenever the living creatures give glory and honor and thanks to Him who sits on the throne, who lives forever and ever, the twenty-four elders fall down before Him who sits on the throne and worship Him who lives forever and ever, and cast their crowns before the throne, saying: "You are worthy, O Lord, to receive glory and honor and power: for You created all things, and by Your will they exist and were created. (Revelation 4:9–11)

What is the response to this tremendous vision in heaven? The response to the true unveiling of the glory and the majesty of God is always submission. Always! Why do people not submit to God? It is because they do not know Him; for to know Him is to immediately fall down in wonder, love, praise, and submission.

In the next chapter, in Revelation 5:8, we find exactly the same thing:

> Now when He had taken the scroll, the four living creatures and the twenty-four elders fell down before the Lamb, each having a harp, and golden bowls full of incense, which are the prayers of the saints.

In Revelation 4 there is the falling down before the One who is on the throne, God Himself. In Revelation 5 there is the falling down before the Lamb, the living Christ. To see God in His glory, that is, to have a glimpse of His glory, is to submit to Him. Just as there can be no true worship of Jesus Christ until there is total submission to Jesus Christ, there can be no true Christianity without submission.

Worship is "worthship," ascribing worth to the one you worship. Notice here that they worship Him as the Creator, for this One on the throne is the Creator. "You are worthy, O Lord," our God.

It is not without significance that this was the title claimed by the Roman emperor at that time. Domitian was to be worshiped and submitted to as lord and god; but there is only one Lord and God, and only He is worthy to receive glory and honor and power. We have seen that these three things are the things that men seek, but only the Creator is worthy of glory and honor and power.

A dear servant of the Lord, Dr. Paul White, was a missionary in Africa until illness caused him to return home. He has written a number of classics on missionary service in Africa under the title *Jungle Doctor*; he is also a most acceptable speaker. On one occasion he gave a message on what it means to be a Christian. He said, "It is something like joining a club. It costs you nothing to join, but your annual dues are all that you have."

Exposition of Revelation 5

One Qualified

> And I saw in the right hand of Him who sat on the throne a scroll written inside and on the back, sealed with seven seals. Then I saw a strong angel proclaiming with a loud voice, "Who is worthy to open the scroll and to loose its seals?" And no one in heaven or on the earth or under the earth was able to open the scroll, or to look at it.
>
> So I wept much, because no one was found worthy to open and read the scroll, or to look at it. But one of the elders said to me, "Do not weep. Behold, the Lion of the tribe of Judah, the Root of David, has prevailed to open the scroll and to loose its seven seals." (Revelation 5:1–5)

The scene changes, and John sees this One with a scroll with writing not only on the front but also on the back, and it is sealed with seven seals. But why seven seals? It is sealed because of the secrets contained in the scrolls, which revealed God's final disposition for the affairs of this world (in other words, that which concerns the future).

And the strong angel cries, "Who is worthy to open the scroll and to loose its seals?" "No one in heaven, or on the earth or under the earth" we are told, "was able to open the scroll, or to look on it." Now "worthy" here seems to imply moral fitness, for moral fitness is the true strength in the heavenly world. Those who are morally fit receive from God the knowledge of God's will.

Why did John weep? He wept because he wanted to understand, and no man was able to open the book and give understanding—not one person in all the universe. There is a tremendous truth here! God will not give His message to a person who is not qualified to receive it.

I am sometimes asked, "Why do you have high school students and college graduates together at the Bible school where you teach?" It is very simple. A college degree does not qualify you for biblical revelation. The Word of God must be revealed by the Spirit of God. There must be the moral qualification. With a college degree you can be trained in your mind, but you have to be prepared in your heart to effectively serve the Lord.

One of the dangers of our time is permitting the academic to displace the spiritual, that is, thinking that academic attainment qualifies us for spiritual revelation. Nothing could be further from the truth. The only thing that qualifies a man for spiritual revelation is moral fitness: a holy life, a life under the control of the Spirit of God, who alone can reveal to him the will of God and enlighten and illumine the Word of God. Moral fitness is the great essential.

The Worthy One Described

In verses 5 and 6, we come to one of the greatest scenes in the book of Revelation:

> But one of the elders said to me, "Do not weep. Behold, the Lion of the tribe of Judah, the Root of David, has prevailed to open the scroll and to loose its seven seals." And I looked, and behold, in the midst of the throne and of the four living creatures, and in the midst of the elders, stood a Lamb as though it had been slain, having seven horns and seven eyes, which are the seven Spirits of God sent out into all the earth.

In this passage we find the Lamb of God coming forward. What a scene! Why is He coming forward? It is because He alone is worthy, primarily because of His victory over death. His worthiness is also revealed in His victory over the powers of darkness, His obedience to His Father, and His spotless life. Therefore, being worthy, He is able to know and to reveal God's secrets. He is also qualified to preside over things to come. What a wonderful Lord He is!

We have seen the Lamb in the midst of the throne coming forth; and He is called by two great titles: the Lion of the tribe of Judah and the Root of David. "The

Lion" speaks of strength and power, the emblem of an all-powerful Messiah. "The Root of David" means that Jesus Christ is the Son of David, the Messiah. So He is the Lion of the tribe of Judah; but notice that He is revealed as the "Lamb as . . . it had been slain" or as a "little lamb." When John looks he sees a little lamb, for the word is diminutive. When we think of a lion, we think of his power, his majesty, his strength; but here is a lamb. Now of what does that speak? It speaks here of power manifested in seeming weakness: a little lamb is in the midst of the throne. How amazing—a lamb, the supreme type of weakness, sitting upon a throne, the supreme symbol of power!

Now the twenty-four elders fall down before the Lamb with seven horns. Here is a different picture given to us to describe the Lamb of God. This is a new conception of the Lamb, a new picture. Whenever we read of a horn or horns in the Bible, it always speaks of power. The seven horns stand for perfect power, or omnipotence. Then we read He had seven eyes. Not only is He omnipotent but also omniscient. These seven eyes stand for the all-seeing omniscience of the Lamb of God. So we have the Lamb of God coming forth with seven horns, which speak of complete power, but also with seven eyes, which reveal to us that the Lamb of God has perfect knowledge and is present in every place—omnipotent, omniscient, omnipresent.

Thus the total picture is the Lamb brought before us as the Lion of the tribe of Judah, the Root of David, the promised Messiah, the One who has all power and all knowledge. He is the One whose all-conquering power none can withstand and whose all-seeing eye none can escape.

Three Great Choruses

In verses 7–14, we have three great choruses to this Lamb: verses 9–10, 11–12, and 13.

> Then He came and took the scroll out of the right hand of him who sat on the throne.
>
> Now when he had taken the scroll, the four living creatures and the twenty-four elders fell down before the Lamb, each having a harp, and golden bowls full of incense, which are the prayers of the saints. (vv. 7–8)

We will remember that the four beasts represent creation, and the elders represent all believers. They are before the Lamb, who holds the secret of life's meaning in His hand. The exalted Christ, the all-knowing, all-powerful Lamb, is central. And what is the response to this vision of the Lamb of God? Again, it is worship.

Why do people not worship God? Why do people not worship the Lamb? It is because they have never had a true vision of the Lamb or a true concept of God, for to know Him is to worship Him.

Then we find that the elders have harps and golden vials "full of incense, which are the prayers of the saints." The harp, of course, was the great instrument in the Old Testament on which the praises of God were played. It aided the one who played it to sing the praises of God.

This is a very beautiful picture of the offering up of the prayers of the saints. As these twenty-four elders are prostrate before this tremendous revelation of the power, might, majesty, and glory of the Lamb of God, they sing a new song, the first of the three great choruses.

> And they sang a new song, saying: "You are worthy to take the scroll, and to open its seals; for you were slain, and have redeemed us to God by Your blood out of every tribe and tongue and people and nation, and have made us kings and priests to our God; and we shall reign on the earth." (vv. 9–10)

This is the greatest song of praise the universe will ever hear, the song of the redeemed. This chorus begins with the four living creatures and the twenty-four elders praising Him because of His worth, because He was slain, because He was crucified. He has redeemed to God by His blood those praising Him out of every kindred and tongue and people and nation. Notice the universality of it all: every tribe, every tongue, every people, every nation.

Notice too the rising chorus of praise by angels in verses 11–12:

> And I looked, and I heard the voice of many angels around the throne, the living creatures, and the elders; and the number of them was ten thousand times ten thousand, and thousands of thousands, saying with a loud voice: "Worthy is the Lamb who

was slain to receive power and riches and wisdom,
and strength and honor and glory and blessing!"

The numbers are not to be taken as literal. It is an innumerable company of angels that sing the second chorus. We hear the voice of many angels and the elders in verse 12 singing the sevenfold, perfect doxology.

Then there is a final chorus of the universe in verse 13. It is more than animate creation worshiping; it is the whole creation.

And every creature which is in heaven and on the earth and under the earth and such as are in the sea, and all that are in them, I heard saying, "Blessing and honor and glory and power be to him who sits on the throne, and to the Lamb, forever and ever."

The Hebrew mind delighted in speaking of every bird, blade of grass, mountain, and river praising and worshiping God. So here we have the whole creation joining in this magnificent chorus, revealing to us God's ultimate purpose in creation. What is it? *God's ultimate purpose is that every created being might worship the One upon the throne and the Lamb upon the throne with Him.* Is that purpose being fulfilled in us? Are we numbered among those who know what it is to praise the One on the throne and to praise the Lamb on the throne with Him?

Here then is the song of the redeemed, echoed by the angels, and now merged into an utterance of all. First the redeemed and then the angels sing this mighty chorus, and then it comes from all quarters and from all forms of creation. The whole creation, animate and inanimate, offers praise and worship.

In the worshiping of Him never forget that it is for all people, all tribes, all tongues, and all nations; for when He reveals Himself to you as the Lamb of God, slain for all, the Spirit of God will create within you a passion that all might know Him.

The first two songs are in honor of the Lamb, but in this last chorus the praise is addressed to both the Enthroned One and the Lamb. This linking of both throughout Revelation is common, but here they are linked in praise. Equal worship and equal honor are given to both, for they are One in deity.

And now we come, in verse 14, to the wonderful conclusion to all this praise of the Lamb and the One who is on the throne:

> Then the four living creatures said, "Amen!" And the twenty-four elders fell down and worshiped Him who lives for ever and ever.

And the four beasts kept saying, "Amen." After each of the ascriptions—"blessing . . . honor . . . glory and power"—this great "Amen!" peals forth. Each ascription glorifies the Lamb—followed by a pause, and the resounding "Amen!" ringing forth, until the worship is complete.

Ev'ry kindred, tongue and nation,
Worthy the Lamb;
Join to sing the great salvation, Worthy the Lamb.
Loud as mighty thunders roaring,
Loud as mighty waters pouring,
Prostrate at His feet adoring,
Worthy the Lamb.

Note

1. See Exodus 19:16–20.

To stretch my hand and touch Him,
Though He be far away;
To raise my eyes and see Him
Through darkness and through day;
To lift my voice and call Him—
This is to pray!

SAMUEL W. DUFFIELD

5

The How of Worship

The severest discipline of a Christian's life is to learn
how to keep "beholding as in a glass the glory of the
Lord." —OSWALD CHAMBERS

Having laid a foundation, we are now prepared to
examine the *how* of worship. How do we worship?
What do we do? First there must be a whole heart, for
true worship is heart worship. If that condition is not
met, there can be no acceptable approach to God.

Then there must be clean hands. There can be no unconfessed sin. We cannot walk in darkness and have fellowship with or worship the One who is in the light, for
unconfessed sin forfeits access to God in worship. There
can be no true worship without obedience.

The Priority of Worship

If you ask most people what prayer is, they would
say, "Prayer is asking God to do something," or, "It is petition," or, "It is supplication," or, "It is intercession." Some
might say that it includes thanksgiving, but generally the
opinion of most would be that we ask God for something
when we come to pray. We have almost ig-
nored the priority of worship.

The following word studies on
prayer by Griffith Thomas bring
into sharp relief the primacy of
worship.

1. Prayer is a sense of need (*deesis* and *deomai* and their cognates). The substantive *deesis* occurs nineteen times and the verb *deomai* twenty-three times. . . . This is, perhaps, the most elementary idea of prayer. . . .

2. Prayer is an *expression of desire* (*aiteo, aitema*). The Greek words are found altogether in some seventy-four passages.

3. Prayer is *a spirit of humility*. This aspect of prayer comes before us in one passage only (Heb. 5:7) where the word *iketeria* refers to our Lord's prayer in Gethsemane, and is translated in our Authorized Version "supplications." . . .

4. Prayer is an *attitude of consecration*. In no less than 125 passages of the New Testament we find the words *proseuche* and *proseuchomai* used to express the idea of prayer. It is by far the commonest word denoting prayer to God, and its root idea is consecration. It is compounded of *euche*, "a vow" and "pros," "turning towards"; and means the turning of ourselves to God in surrender. It *is an attitude of worship expressed in prayer* [italics added].

5. Prayer is a *privilege of fellowship*. This thought is suggested by the rare word *enteuxis* which occurs only twice in the New Testament (1 Tim. 2:1; 4:5), being rendered "intercession" in the former, and "prayer" in the latter passage.

6. Prayer is a *spirit of enquiry.* The word suggesting
   this is *erotuo* (John 16:23) . . . This word is used
   once in the New Testament in connection with
   prayer.
7. Prayer is *a bond of union.* In Matthew 18:19 we
   read, "If two of you agree on earth concerning
   anything that they ask." The word translated
   "agree" is "sum phoneo," from which we get our
   word "symphony."[1]

As Thomas notes in point 4, the 125 references in
the New Testament to *proseuche or proseuchomai* for
"consecration" indicates an attitude of worship should be
part of our prayers. Through "the large number of occur-
rences of these [two] words we can readily see what is
the normal attitude of the believer in prayer," he writes.
"It is the attitude of a worshipper, of one who is turned
towards God with all his heart and soul."[2]

Bishop Westcott was one of the truly outstanding
biblical scholars of his time. He was also a humble man.
When he went in his carriage to the city of Durham, he
would never face the people, but always rode with his
back to them. He said he was not worthy; and yet, here
was one of the great Greek scholars of his time and a
mighty man of God.

It was his son who said of Westcott, "In his final years
my father obviously lived in two worlds at once. Whilst
his feet were set in the earth, his spirit was in the presence of God. Everything that came to him was met in

that presence. Nothing could ever surprise him from that attitude."[3]

He had mastered the art of unceasing worship, the fruit of which was an unceasing consciousness of the presence of his Lord. It is difficult, yes, but possible.

Preparing for Worship

Aloneness

You enter your closet; and a closet, you will recall, is a closed place. It may be your bedroom, your study, or that place in your home that you have set apart. It could be a garden or a field. Whatever becomes your closet, it is there that you meet the Lord every morning; and your objective is fellowship in aloneness with a consciously present Lord. This should be first and completely separate from a time of Bible study and intercession. You will recall our Lord's first lesson on prayer as found in Matthew: "When you pray, go into your room ["closet" KJV], and when you have shut your door, pray to your Father who is in the secret place; and your Father who sees in secret will reward you openly." (6:6). A study of the verse reveals the use of the singular pronoun no less than eight times, emphasizing how personal and intimate is this first lesson.

Sin

Entering into our closet demands a true heart and no unconfessed sin. We should not wait until our quiet time to deal with sin. Sin should be dealt with immediately. If we are conscious of having grieved or quenched the

Spirit or having done that which is not pleasing in His sight, we must stop wherever we are and confess our sin. This should not take more than thirty seconds. We dare not leave the confession of our sin for that early morning worship.

D. L. Moody knew what it was to keep "short accounts" with God, but he also developed an excellent practice. Every evening before retiring he would review the day with his Lord, trusting Him to reveal anything that had displeased Him. Such a man is prepared for worship.

The Holy Spirit

We must come with dependence on the Holy Spirit who wants to draw out our hearts in worship, but this can only be as we learn to restfully depend on Him. Philippians 3:3 speaks eloquently of the ministry of the Spirit in worship: "We are the circumcision," says Paul, "who worship God in the spirit."

Beck translates it "We who worship by God's spirit." True worship, therefore, is only possible when the spirit of man is controlled by the Spirit of God. For as Arthur Pink well said, "We can no more pray without the Holy Spirit than we can create a world."

Concentration

We enter our closet, shut the door behind us, and are alone with our Lord. We kneel, with our eyes closed in order to concentrate all our attention and affection on the Lamb of God, forgetting all else in order not to forget Him.

I have shared with you the great discovery I made in my quiet time when I began to concentrate all my attention on the slain Lamb of God. When you first attempt this you may experience turmoil. Numerous thoughts may race through your mind along with a multitude of things that need your attention. You must trust the Spirit of God to enable you to concentrate all your attention and affection on the Lamb of God. Do not give up.

The Practice of Worship

Express your ascriptions of worth to Him audibly. Pray aloud.

Using Scripture

Use the words of Scripture, and make them your own. For example, recall that wonderful verse in Revelation 5:9: "You are worthy to take the scroll, and to open its seals; for you were slain, and have redeemed us to God by Your blood."

Now how would you adapt that to worship? Lift your heart to the Lord and say to Him: "You are worthy to take the scroll, and to open its seals; for you were slain, and have redeemed *me* to God by Your blood." The word must be intensely personal and adapted for your own use.

Revelation 5:12 can be adapted as follows: "*You* are worthy to receive power and riches, and wisdom, and strength and honor and glory and blessing!"

The Psalms, of course, abound with worship. For example, the first verse of Psalm 8 is readily adapted to worship. But how? The psalmist says, "O Lord, our Lord, how excellent is Your name in all the earth."

To adapt one would say, "O Lord my Lord, how excellent is Your name in all the earth!" The worship need not be in the exact words of the Psalms. One can develop worship using the sense of the words in a prayer such as the following:

> O Lord, You are my Lord; for You in Your mercy and wondrous grace did redeem me. You purchased me. You plucked my feet out of the net. You reconciled me to Yourself. O Lord, my Lord, how excellent is Your wondrous Name to me. You who have set Your glory above the heavens did give Your own beloved Son to a cross. You set Him forth to be a propitiation for my sin. O Lord, my Lord, how excellent is Your Name in all the earth.

Turn to Psalm 19:1: "The heavens declare the glory of God; and the firmament shows His handiwork." How are you going to adapt that? "The heavens declare *Your* glory, and the firmament shows *Your* handiwork." This is worship.

Then there's Psalm 36:5–9, which begins,

> Your mercy, O Lord, is in the heavens; Your faithfulness reaches to the clouds. Your righteousness is like the great mountains; Your judgments are a great deep; O Lord, You preserve man and beast. (vv. 5–6)

That is worship. You are ascribing worth to God. Verses 7–9 can be adapted as follows:

> How precious is Your lovingkindness, O God! Therefore the children of men put their trust under the shadow of Your wings. They are abundantly satisfied with the fullness of Your house, and You give them drink of Your pleasures. For with You is the fountain of life; in Your light we see light.

Look at Psalm 29:1: "Give unto the Lord, O you mighty ones, give unto the Lord glory and strength." How would you adapt that? This one is not as simple. "*I* give unto *You*, O Lord, *for You are* mighty. I give unto *You* O Lord, glory and strength." Do you see how it must be personalized?

Verse 2 reads,

> Give unto the Lord the glory due to his name.

But we would want to say, "I *would* give unto *You*, O Lord, the glory due unto *Your* name."

The adaptation of Psalm 90:1 is simple. "Lord, You have been our dwelling place in all generations" would become "You have been my dwelling place." Are you going to say "in all generations"? No. "You have been my dwelling place, *wondrous Lord, since that first day when my chains fell off and my heart was free*." Verse 2 does not need adapting: "Before the mountains were brought forth, or ever You had formed the earth and the world, even from everlasting to everlasting, You are God."

What do you notice about these passages of Scripture in which you worship? There is occupation with Him. Is not the first great commandment to "love the Lord thy God with all thy heart"? (Mark 12:28–30a KJV). In worship you are completely occupied with the One you love. You are unmindful of self or anybody or anything else. This is essential in true worship.

Again, Psalm 93:1 proclaims, "The Lord reigns, He is clothed with majesty; *the* Lord is clothed, He has girded Himself with strength." How can that be adapted? Remember it must be intensely personal. "*You*, Lord, reign. *You are* clothed with majesty. *You are* clothed, girded with strength.

Then again, Psalm 104:1 says, "Bless the Lord, O my soul! O Lord my God, You are very great: You are clothed with honor and majesty." How would we adapt these verses? "I *would bless You, wondrous Lord. I would bless You. I would bless You with all my soul, for You are my* Lord *and* my God. You are very great. You are clothed with honor and majesty."

Some verses do not need adaptation, such as Psalm 139:1–4:

> O Lord, You have searched me and known me. *You* know my sitting down and my rising up; You understand my thought afar off. *You comprehend* my path and my lying down, and are acquainted with all my ways. For there is not a word on my tongue, but

behold, O Lord, *You* know it altogether. [Emphasis added]

When you use these passages of Scripture, begin by simply reading them to the Lord; but you need to memorize them. Set yourself the task of memorizing one verse a week; and when you come to your time of worship, you will find the Spirit of God using the memorized Scriptures to draw out your heart in worship.

Using Hymns

Hymns also are a wonderful aid. Until we published our own hymnal at the Evangelical Institute, I used two hymnals. The *InterVarsity Fellowship Hymnal* (IVF) is rather small. If you can obtain it, the *Keswick Hymnal* is better; but, unfortunately, it is out of print. It is not that the selections are superior, but it is much larger. Let us consider some of the great hymns of worship. Remember that they must be a direct ascription of praise, and they must be intensely personal.

"Holy, Holy, Holy" is a hymn of worship.

Holy, Holy, Holy! Lord God Almighty!
Early in the morning our song shall rise to Thee;
Holy, Holy, Holy! Merciful and Mighty!
God in Three Persons, blessed Trinity!

This is worship. Memorize the hymn, making the words your own.

Some of the happiest moments of my life were spent

in Japan with our first daughter, Elizabeth. When she was about three and a half years old, I would often take her with me to the nearby town. As we would bump along together in our little Volkswagen over the rough road, I taught her this hymn. It was the first hymn she memorized. Why? It is because, even though a small child three and a half years old, she must learn and never forget one thing: she was created to worship God. I can still hear that little voice singing, "Cherubim and seraphim." What music to a father's ears! How pleasing to the ears of our Lord!

Another worshipful hymn is "Fairest Lord Jesus."

Fairest Lord Jesus! Ruler of all nature,
O Thou of God and man the Son!
Thee will I cherish, Thee will I honor,
Thou, my soul's glory, joy and crown.

This is worship. Here is verse two:

Fair are the meadows, fairer still the woodlands,
Robed in the blooming garb of spring;
Jesus is fairer, Jesus is purer,
Who makes the woeful heart to sing.

Adapt the second stanza to say,

Fair are the meadows, fairer still the woodlands,
Robed in the blooming garb of spring;

Jesus, Thou art fairer, Jesus, *Thou* art purer,
For *Thou hast made my* woeful heart to sing.

Then there is a hymn not quite so direct, but a beautiful one: "Thee Will I Love, My Strength, My Tower."

Thee will I love, my Strength, my Tower,
Thee will I love, my Joy, my Crown,
Thee will I love 'til sacred fire
Fills my whole soul with pure desire.

How would you adapt this to make it a prayer?

Precious Lord, Thou art worthy of all my love, all my strength, all my power. Thou art worthy to be loved and loved alone above all others; for Thou art my joy, Thou art my crown, Thou art my all.

Then there is the wonderful hymn, "And Can It Be That I Should Gain?" by Charles Wesley.

And can it be that I should gain
An interest in the Saviour's blood?
Died He for me, who caused His pain?
For me, who Him to death pursued?
Amazing love! How can it be
That Thou, my God, shouldst die for me?

This is one of the greatest hymns of all time. How would you adapt it? It is not a simple hymn to adapt, but it can be done.

And can it be, *dear Lord*, that I should gain
An interest in *Thy precious* blood?
Did *You die* for me who caused Your pain?
For me, *who pursued You* to death?
Amazing love! How can it be
That Thou, my God, should die for me?

The third stanza:

He left His Father's throne above,
So free, so infinite His grace;
Emptied Himself of all but love,
And bled for Adam's helpless race;
Tis mercy all, immense and free;
 For, O my God, it found out me.

Adapting this verse you could say,

Thou didst leave *Thy* Father's throne above,
So free, so infinite *Thy* grace;
Thou didst empty *Thyself* of all but love,
And bled for Adam's helpless race.
Wondrous Lord, 'tis mercy all, *so* immense, *so* free;
And *O dear Lord*, it found out me!

A favorite hymn that I invariably use in my time of
worship is "Eternal Light! Eternal Light!" Whenever I
am a little tired, and tiredness can be an enemy to true

worship, I slowly use the words of this hymn to tune my
heart. It never fails.

> Eternal light! Eternal Light!
> How pure the soul must be
> When, placed within Thy searching sight,
> It shrinks not, but with calm delight
> Can live, and look on Thee!

Such a stanza can inspire the following:

> Thou who art Light, dwelling in light unapproachable,
> how can I come before Thee?
> Thou art of purer eyes than to behold iniquity.
> My purity is as filthy rags in Thy sight;
> but in Thy Son I am beheld as He is,
> for He is my purity.
> Therefore, I come in Him before Thee boldly;
> for Thou has bid me come.
> With calm delight I may live and look on Thee.

A final hymn easily adaptable for worship is "Gracious
God, We Worship Thee."

> Gracious God, we worship Thee,
> Rev'rently we bow the knee;
> Jesus Christ our only plea:
> Father, we adore Thee.

> Vast Thy love, how deep, how wide,
> In the gift of Him who died

Righteous claims all satisfied:
Father, we adore Thee.

Low we bow before Thy face,
Sons of God, O wondrous place;
Great the riches of Thy grace:
Father, we adore Thee.

By Thy Spirit grant that we
Worshippers in truth may be;
Praise, as incense sweet to Thee:
Father, we adore Thee.

Yet again our song we raise,
Note of deep adoring praise;
Now, and soon through endless days:
Father, we adore Thee.

In adapting these stanzas one might say:

Gracious God, *I* worship Thee,
Rev'rently *I* bow the knee;
Jesus Christ *my* only plea:
Father, *I* adore Thee.

Vast Thy love, how deep, how wide,
In the gift of Him who died;
Righteous claims all satisfied:
Father, *I* adore Thee.

Low I bow before Thy face,
Son of God, O wondrous place;
Great the riches of Thy grace:
Father, I adore Thee.

By Thy Spirit grant that I
A *worshiper* in truth may be;
Praise, as incense sweet to Thee:
Father, *I* adore Thee.

Yet again *My* song I raise,
Note of deep adoring praise;
Now, and soon through endless days:
Father, I adore Thee.

The Christian Book of Mystical Verse, by A. W. Tozer, is valuable for meditation and use in your time of worship. In it you will find a precious word by John Bowring:

Almighty One! I bend in dust before Thee;
Even so veiled cherubs bend;
In calm and still devotion I adore Thee,
All-wise, all-present Friend!
Thou to the earth its emerald robes hast given,
Or curtained it in snow;
And the bright sun, and the soft moon in heaven,
Before Thy presence bow.[4]

Then too there is the inspiring poem "The Unity of God," by Frederick William Faber.

One God! one Majesty!
There is no God but Thee!
Unbounded, unextended Unity!
Awful in unity,
O God! we worship Thee,
More simply one, because supremely Three!
Unfathomable Sea!
All life is out of Thee,
And Thy life is Thy blissful Unity.

Blest be thy Unity!
All joys are one to me,
The joy that there can be no other God than Thee![5]

One should never overlook Gerhard Tersteegen's
"God Reveals His Presence."

God reveals His presence:
Let us now adore Him,
And with awe appear before Him.
God is in His temple;
All within keep silence,
Prostrate lie with deepest reverence.
Him alone,
God we own,
Him our God and Savior:
Praise His Name for ever![6]

Tersteegen's verse may be adapted in this way:

Thou hast revealed Thy presence:
I would now adore *Thee*,
And with awe appear before *Thee.*
Thou art in *Thy* temple;
I would within keep silence,
Prostrate lie with deepest reverence.
Thou alone
My God I own,
Thee, my God and Saviour:
Praise *Thy* Name for ever!

Using Books

In his day no man has understood worship as A. W. Tozer, for he knew what it was to worship God. In 1952, when Dr. Tozer was invited to take a series of meetings at Wheaton College, I was asked to counsel with inquiring students. Hesitating in my acceptance, I asked why Dr. Tozer would not do so. I was told that he required two and a half hours of prayer for every hour that he preached. Since he would be preaching for two hours daily, he would need five hours in prayer. I immediately accepted the invitation.

The one book you must obtain by A. W. Tozer is *The Knowledge of the Holy*,[7] a small volume on the attributes of God. One of the great lacks of our time is a true knowledge of God. What is He like, this wonderful Being? We cannot even define Him; but as we study His attributes, we can see "even as through a glass darkly" something of the wonder of the Person we worship. There is no book in print that will give you such a graphic introduction to the attributes of God. Summarize each chapter until you are able to grasp its meaning. I believe that will bring you as quickly as possible into a knowledge of what God is like.

Two other books by Dr. Tozer—*Worship* and *The Pursuit of God*[8]—will also inspire and aid you in your worship.

Another worthy volume on worship is by A. P. Gibbs entitled *Worship*.[9] There also is a small chapter on worship in John Stott's *Christ the Controversialist*.[10] More recently, Dr. John MacArthur's volume, *Worship: The Ultimate Priority*,[11] is excellent. These books can be invaluable in your study of worship.

Hindrances to Worship

We need to carefully consider the following six hindrances, for to ignore them is to forfeit a consistent experience of satisfying worship.

Unsurrendered Heart

The first hindrance is an unsurrendered heart. There is no such thing as a once-for-all surrender, for did not our Lord say, "If anyone desires to come after me, let him deny himself, and take up his cross daily, and follow me" (Luke 9:23)?

Here we are confronted with a crisis followed by a process, but when does the crisis take place? "If anyone will come after me, let him deny himself. . . ." The crisis is the dethroning of Self and the enthroning of Christ. This is followed by a process: the daily cross, the daily dethroning of Self that Christ may remain enthroned. You never cease to surrender. You must maintain the attitude of a surrendered heart, or you will drift away and yield to competing affections. Suddenly you realize that you are not getting through to the Lord in your time of worship, and you are in dire peril of not really wanting to worship. Keep your heart surrendered and tender toward the Lord.

Unconfessed Sin

The second hindrance of course is unconfessed sin. Do not think your unconfessed sin will simply go away. It will not. It will no more go away than cancer will disappear. Sin is a cancer, and it must be dealt with. Remember to keep a short account through confession of sin. Confess it immediately, calling it by its worst name. Repent, and go on with your Lord.

Wrong Attitude

The third hindrance to worship is a wrong attitude, especially when it is directed toward a brother or sister in the body of Christ. When we have wrong attitudes, we grieve the Spirit of God. If this condition exists, it is impossible to worship God. Watch your attitudes very carefully, and deal ruthlessly with them by needful confession and repentance.

Enemy Opposition

There may be times when an oppressive cloud will come to distract you. Refuse it in the name of Jesus. "Therefore submit to God. Resist the devil, and he will flee from you" (James 4:7). This oppression is much more common on mission fields, but you can also experience it in America. Do not be deceived into thinking a sudden heaviness of spirit is because of some undealt with sin. It is invariably the enemy.

Physical Tiredness

The fifth hindrance to worship is physical tiredness. I have found a cold morning shower helpful. It is also of first importance to obtain sufficient sleep. John Wesley would excuse himself each evening with the words, "It is now ten o'clock. I must retire. I have an appointment at four in the morning with my Lord." Consistent physical exercise, especially walking, is a must. Guard also against emotional fatigue, for this will cause a more debilitating tiredness than most any other factor.

Unbelief

Unbelief is the sixth hindrance. When you prepare yourself for worship, faith is foremost. You must believe that you are going to have a wonderful time with the Lord.

It was my privilege on one occasion to meet a true worshiper of the Lord in Scotland. Her name was Mrs. Stewart, a lovable sister of humble origin. She sustained herself by cleaning offices in a part of Scotland where women still get down on their knees and scrub floors.

When I visited Scotland with my wife, I said, "We must see Mrs. Stewart because she has been praying for me every day for many years."

We went to her lowly dwelling, just two rooms and

a little kitchen with a mirror on the wall that divided the rooms. One room was her bedroom, and the other was her living room.

As she passed from her bedroom to the living room early each morning, she would look in the mirror. Why? Her reply was revealing. "You know, I worship my Lord in the living room; but when I come out of my bedroom, I pass by this mirror and make a final check of myself because I want to look my best for my lovely Lord."

This woman knew her Lord intimately. I would have given much to hear her worship Jesus Christ. There was no doubt in her mind that she was going to see her Lord, and she wanted to look her best.

Lostness in Worship

It was my privilege to serve in the Australian army for six years during the long war that began in September 1939. During that time of World War II, I met some fine Christians; there were not many, but some were exceptional men of God. The most outstanding by far was a young man named Tom Walton.

I was present the night Tom was converted in an army training camp hut. The chaplain preached a powerful gospel message, and following his appeal there was the "thud, thud, thud" of the hobnail boots of a young man coming to the front. I looked up and saw a rosy-cheeked fellow with big horn-rimmed glasses making his way forward to surrender all to Christ as Lord.

I thought, I *wonder if he will really stand*? The Australian army was not a place for weaklings. But stand he did.

Young Tom was sent as a reinforcement to one of our oldest divisions, which had fought in Africa. Such old soldiers were loath to accept the green reinforcement, but young Tom won their hearts when he "laid his life on the line" and was decorated for bravery in his very first engagement with his unit.

When he was killed, six weeks before the Armistice, those hardened veterans wept uncontrollably. They had lost their "Christian," whom they loved dearly.

On one occasion I went to the commanding officer of his unit and requested that, as they had recently been in action for a long period, Tom might spend a few days with me.

The officer said, "Walton? Walton? Oh, you mean Christian."

"Well, I don't know what you call him; but he is Tom Walton," I said.

"Yes, well, we call him Christian."

Why did they call him Christian? What made Tom so different that the whole battalion knew of him and respected him highly? The answer is simple. Our young soldier of Jesus Christ had made the worship of his Lord the first thing in his life.

I read his diary after the war. It was not unusual to find statements such as, "We attack at dawn. I will be up at four o'clock to worship my Lord."

One morning he was absent from parade when his name was called; and the officer said to the sergeant, "Where is Walton?"

He answered, "I do not know, Sir."

Finding Tom, the sergeant said, "Walton! Walton! We're on parade! Get on parade! What is the matter, man?"

So Tom very quickly put on his equipment and made his way to the parade ground. Three or four days later the same thing happened again.

"Where is Walton, Sergeant?" "I do not know."

"Well, go and find him."

So the sergeant went to Tom's tent, and there was Tom on his knees, praying. The officer said, "If this happens again, Walton, I will have to parade you before the colonel."

It did happen again; and this time he was taken up before the colonel who, of course, had decorated the boy and knew him.

"Three times you have been absent from parade," said the colonel. "This is not a good example for a corporal. Christian, this is not like you. What's wrong?"

Tom in his beautiful, sweet way said, "Well, Colonel, I begin to worship my Lord Jesus (he used to call Him his beautiful Lord Jesus); and I cannot hear anything. I do not hear the bugle. I do not hear the men. I do not hear anything. I'm sorry."

Tom had reached that rare plateau of lostness in the worship of his Lord. The rattle of equipment, the shrill peal of the bugle, the noise of running feet—he was oblivious to it all.

At nineteen years of age Tom Walton was in action in Borneo when suddenly—he was not, for God took him.

Notes

1. W. H. Griffith Thomas, *Life Abiding and Abounding* (Chicago: Bible Institute Colportage Association, 1910), 33–41. All italics added.

2. Ibid., 37.

3. Quoted in G. H. Morling, *Quest for Serenity* (Grand Rapids: Eerdmans, 1965), 36.

4. A. W. Tozer, *The Christian Book of Mystical Verse* (Harrisburg, Pa.: Christian Publications, 1963), 2–3. Originally published in *Hymns for the Church of Christ* (n. p., 1857), 74.

5. Ibid., 3–4.

6. Ibid., 60.

7. A. W. Tozer, *The Knowledge of the Holy* (New York: Harper and Row, 1961).

8. A. W. Tozer, *Worship* (Harrisburg, PA: Christian Publications, 1961); *The Pursuit of God* (Harrisburg, PA: Christian Publications, 1948; repr. Camp Hill PA, 1982).

9. Alfred P. Gibbs, *Worship* (Fort Dodge, Iowa: Walterick, n.d.; repr. Dubuque Iowa: ECS Ministries, 2013), www.ecministries.org.

10. *Christ the Controversialist* (Downers Grove, Ill.: InterVarsity), 1974.

11. John MacArthur, *Worship: The Ultimate Priority* (Chicago: Moody, 2012).